What readers are saying about *From Java to Ruby*

Bruce has a great reputation as a forward-leaning thinker, and he articulates his opinions well. The mix of audience (Manager and Developer) leans towards managers, but he manages to pull this difficult mix off well. It is just as good as I would expect from Bruce, having read his other works.

▶ **Neal Ford**
  Author, speaker, and architect, Thoughtworks

Many leading developers are already sold on the idea that Ruby can benefit their organizations—however, most of us still have to convince our management. With Bruce Tate's *Java to Ruby*, we have a powerful ally in our quest to add this fantastic language to our toolbox.

▶ **Nathaniel T. Schutta**
  Co-author, Foundations of Ajax

This is a book that every die hard Java developer should read. The strategy of integrating current Java Enterprise assets with Ruby's productivity can bring the edge that an organization needs to remain competitive, react quicker to requirements, market shifts and ultimately more agile.

▶ **Miguel Serrano**
  Enterprise Architect, VWR International

This book provides an excellent overview of the important Ruby components and concepts to the Java developer.

▶ **Jeffrey Blessing, Ph.D.**
  Professor, Milwaukee School of Engineering

From Java to Ruby

Things Every Manager Should Know

From Java to Ruby

Things Every Manager Should Know

Bruce Tate

The Pragmatic Bookshelf
Raleigh, North Carolina   Dallas, Texas

Many of the designations used by manufacturers and sellers to distinguish their products are claimed as trademarks. Where those designations appear in this book, and The Pragmatic Programmers, LLC was aware of a trademark claim, the designations have been printed in initial capital letters or in all capitals. The Pragmatic Starter Kit, The Pragmatic Programmer, Pragmatic Programming, Pragmatic Bookshelf and the linking *g* device are trademarks of The Pragmatic Programmers, LLC.

Every precaution was taken in the preparation of this book. However, the publisher assumes no responsibility for errors or omissions, or for damages that may result from the use of information (including program listings) contained herein.

Our Pragmatic courses, workshops, and other products can help you and your team create better software and have more fun. For more information, as well as the latest Pragmatic titles, please visit us at

```
http://www.pragmaticprogrammer.com
```

ISBN 0-9766940-9-3

Printed on acid-free paper with 85% recycled, 30% post-consumer content.

First printing, June 2006

Version: 2006-5-23

Contents

The enemy of the truth is very often not the lie—deliberate, contrived, and dishonest—but the myth—persistent, persuasive, and unrealistic.
► John F. Kennedy

Preface

The Explosion

When I started writing *From Java to Ruby*, I had a good idea that Java was not the perfect solution for every problem, though some in the industry may wish it were so. I knew Java visionaries were nervously abandoning Java as they began to recognize real productivity problems and unrelenting complexity. I saw the Java community suffer through an unreal proliferation of frameworks, providing new choices but also introducing an integration quagmire and a near-paralyzing uncertainty. I heard from Java customers flailing against the tide of increasing complexity, desperate to keep their heads above water. In truth, some of those customers needed Java, and many still do. Still, others used Java because it was the popular platform at the time, even though more suitable alternatives existed. With slowly building momentum behind Ruby on Rails, I saw Ruby as a good candidate for growth. If Ruby kept growing, *From Java to Ruby* might have a chance.

But I had no idea how violent the explosion could be. Since I started writing this book, I've seen Ruby on Rails downloads grow by nearly an order of magnitude. Where I used to get dozens of emails a day, I now sometimes get hundreds of emails in a few hours from the Rails support forums. You can get books, hosting, training, consulting, and informed opinions from many reputable sources. Make no mistake: Ruby is exploding, and developers are driving the revolution. Developers can see the simplicity and power of Ruby, and developers first experience the amazing productivity improvements when using Rails.

The problem is this: developers don't usually pick technologies or sign checks. If Ruby is to continue the rapid growth, we developers need to understand how to make an effective case for our technology—but not by using technical buzzwords. We need to communicate in the language our managers understand.

Those deciding between Java and Ruby must understand how Ruby can save them money and help them better satisfy the needs of their customers.

I now believe that the ideas expressed in this book fill a vacuum. If this programmer-led revolution is to advance into the enterprise where it can do the most good, we must learn to express how the technical advantages of Ruby help solve business problems in ways that Java can't. After interviewing customers, visionaries, and Ruby programmers for this book I am more convinced than ever that Ruby represents a fundamental advancement over Java for many of the most important problems we need to solve. In *From Java to Ruby*, you'll learn:

- Why the Ruby risk profile is decreasing, even as Java's rapidly accelerates.

- Where Ruby can help, where it can't, and where it simply has more growing to do.

- Pilot strategies others have successfully used across many industries and circumstances.

- What industry visionaries say about Ruby.

If you think you might want to consider Ruby, other books may concentrate on helping you express your Java programs in Ruby. This book is about moving minds. If you are a manager, *From Java to Ruby* will help you articulate why Ruby is so important to your project, developers, and your customers. If you are a developer, you can buy this book for your manager or use the ideas to convince him yourself. These ideas work. I've used them successfully to jump-start my Ruby practice, and two reviewers of the book have already used them to help their management teams make the right decisions. They can work for you, too.

Acknowledgments

Writing a book is a challenging endeavor that tests each author with every word. Writing a book worthy of my name, and that of my colleagues at the Pragmatic Bookshelf, takes passion and plenty of help. *From Java to Ruby* would not have been possible without many people who stirred my passion, provided technical support, answered my questions, and provided frank criticism.

I'm profoundly grateful to all who helped. If I fail to mention you, please accept my heartfelt apologies. Please let me know so I can list you here.

In particular, I would like to thank the people who use and drive this emerging language. This book would not be the same without the practical experience each one of you provided. I thank my good friend Stuart Halloway for an excellent discussion about the merits of Ruby. Thanks also to Neal Ford for shaping my thinking, and sharing your network.

Thanks to Martin Fowler for the phone conversations that helped shape my thinking and the subsequent interview that advances the ideas in this book. I'm a huge admirer, and I was more than a little in awe as I interviewed you. Thanks to Joshua Haberman at Amazon.com and Heri ter Steeg for telling your stories about real production applications in Ruby. Your ideas are compelling. I hope they will motivate others to succeed with Ruby as you have.

As an open source community, many developers contribute excellent frameworks and ideas to this community without any compensation. Several of the interviews in this book are by such people. Thanks to David Heinemeier Hansson for your astounding energy leading to the Rails framework. Thanks also for your note setting me straight about how things are accomplished in the Rails world—the note that ultimately led to the interview in this book. I'm thrilled with your creation and learning more about the little things you got right every day. Thanks to Jamis Buck, again, for your contributions to migrations, Capistrano, and base Rails. And thanks for being willing to tell my readers about your experience. You've always been willing to help.

The JRuby project is so exciting to me that I dedicated space for two interviews on the topic. Thanks to Thomas E. Enebo and Charles O. Nutter for your Herculean efforts in actually making Rails run on the JVM. I can't believe I'm actually typing that. Also, thanks for spending so much time with me so I could tell my readers what you've done and for helping me get the details right. I've got high hopes for JRuby from many different perspectives.

Thanks also to all of those who reviewed *From Java to Ruby*: Jeffrey Blessing, Miguel Serrano, Nate Schutta, Robert Brown, Steve Yegge, Venkat Subramanium, and Wesley Reisz. Your comments were often frank. If your ego can survive the experience, these are the types of comments that help a book. I was blown away by the quality of your comments. I built a document with each comment you made, and considered every single one.

This is the first review process I've been through with such good feedback from each and every reviewer. Thanks also to Kim Wimpsett for a thorough copy edit.

I have a special desire to thank Dave and Andy. You both stepped in to do jobs that I'd never expect a typical publisher to do. Then again, nothing about the Pragmatic Bookshelf is the least bit typical. Dave, we've worked the same conference for three years now, and I'm finally getting around to doing a book with you. I should have done it before. The experience has been particularly rewarding to me. You opened doors for me that might still otherwise be closed. It must have been maddening working with some of my early stuff. Thanks for the hours formatting my text and graphics before I got comfortable with my new tool set. Andy, thanks for stepping out of your role and into mine to fill in details and make sure each pixel was in the right place. You've got a fantastic sense for what a book needs. I've not worked with this end of the Pragmatic dynamic duo, and now feel shorted. Individually, you're top notch. As a team, you're amazing to work with. Thanks to both of you for giving me this opportunity and helping me to make the most of it. And thanks for bringing a much needed jolt of sanity to the publishing process. It's nice to see the good guys do well.

More than anyone else, I'd like to thank my family. Julia, you will never know how beautiful you are to me. When you laugh, the whole room laughs with you. Kayla, your smile works magic on my soul. I've been tremendously proud of you both for all you've done at school as dyslexics. Keep working hard. You both know that daddy is dyslexic too, but if I can write a book or two, you can overcome your problems to make words do anything you want. Maggie, through it all, you have been the love of my life and my inspiration. You support me even when you are afraid. You give me joy and laughter even when pressing publishing deadlines make it seem like there's not much to smile or laugh about. You do the little things like proofreading some early disasters, helping me work through copy edits, and anything else that needs doing. More than anything else, you love me. That love feeds my energy and passion for writing. I'd be a worthless author without you. I love you, always and ever.

Bruce Tate
June, 2006
bruce@rapidred.com

Chapter 1

Introduction

As I drove across the central Texas landscape, my excitement and anxiety were both building. I was driving to a new client that would change everything for me. This short trip would take me an hour south to a small college town, but symbolically I was beginning a much longer journey. I was going from Java to Ruby.

The past year, I had been involved in my first non-Java project in more than a decade, and based on that success, I had recently written a book called *Beyond Java*. I called into question my investments in not only the Java platform but also ten years of skills, hundreds of customers, scores of enterprise applications, four Java books (including three Java One best-sellers and a Jolt award), and a reputation as a pragmatic Java developer. As often happens, researching *Beyond Java* changed the way I think about software development today. Modern programming should be about *leverage*, with much more emphasis on total cost and productivity. The more I learned, the more I believed that this industry was heading for a revolution that would change the way we write most database-backed Internet applications first and a much broader suite of applications later. I put together a plan to ready my company for the pending revolution, but planning and executing show much different levels of commitment. This client would be my first full-Ruby client.

I had worked on a small Ruby implementation before, at a small start-up, but as a project manager, I had taken only limited peeks at the Ruby code. At other times, I had also taught some small half-day Ruby classes. This account would be my first large all-Ruby engagement, but I was convinced that Ruby was the right language for my customer, and for me, based on a number of criteria:

- Many of the programmers I respected the most raved about the productivity and beauty of the Ruby language. With the Java language, my productivity had been increasingly restricted under the growing weight of a steady stream of new frameworks. Java began to feel restrictive.

- The Ruby on Rails framework was experiencing explosive growth. I had seen programming languages explode like this only twice over the span of my career, with the introduction of the C++ and Java languages.

- Ruby motivated me. The Ruby language rekindled some fires for the love of programming, which I had not experienced since the early days of Java.

- Ruby on Rails was gaining maturity. As Ruby on Rails kept stacking up a steady stream of achievements, I started to believe that this framework could satisfy the needs of *my* customers.

So I drove through central Texas, contemplating my longer journey, filled with nagging questions. Would Ruby succeed or leave me hanging? Would I be able to fill my calendar with Ruby work, and would I be able to fill the gaps with Java assignments? I knew my customer was having the same kinds of doubts.

1.1 The Emergence of Ruby

As I readied for change, I needed only the right customer. When a company south of Austin invited me to build a Ruby on Rails application with them, I couldn't refuse. The application was a perfect fit for Ruby on Rails, a new database-backed web-enabled application with an existing implementation on Microsoft's .NET Framework. They had pressing cost concerns and scheduling constraints that I did not believe we could meet with existing Java or .NET technologies. I had a project, a motivated client, and all the right conditions for success. I told the customer that Ruby was a match, and we continued.

When I said that I'd be doing demos every week starting the first week after development, the company was plainly skeptical. They doubted that we'd be able to do enough work to justify a room full of clients for a demo, but as we presented the first week's demo, the skepticism was replaced with excitement. The Rails language let us quickly generate some basic business objects, carve out our security model, and get the first dozen or so screens up to show our users. With some of the application in hand, we had a common basis for real communication. Everyone in the room was aware that this project would be different.

After only two days of training, my development team, consisting of two Ruby novices, started writing code the first day, and they continued to improve through the first month. By the second month, they were fully productive members of a well-oiled machine. The first four demos included work that the customer estimated would take them four months on the Java platform. For the customer, genuine excitement replaced skepticism, and my biggest challenge was controlling the scope creep born of months of accumulated requirements that they had been unable to work into their existing system.

After three months worth of development, we had completed the development phase, with a few minor exceptions. We had put aside a month for testing and ironing out development issues. We had handled the development twice as fast and with less than a quarter of the cost of the existing implementation. The new application was faster, provided a much better user interface, and included many capabilities that the original version could not possibly touch. My customer now believed, and I validated my own belief. As *From Java to Ruby* readies for production, our application also readies for production. All early indications are good except for a few typical growing pains.

As a mountain biker and white-water kayaker, hard decisions are familiar to me. I'm often perched at the top of a dangerous drop on land or water, deciding whether the trail or rapid is worth the risk and the best way to attack it. I have to understand the potential rewards of the move and weigh those against the unavoidable risks. I have to take steps to mitigate that risk and be able to recover should the need arise.

Shifting the foundation of my practice from Java to Ruby was exactly the same. I needed to understand the consequences of failure, measure those against the potential rewards, mitigate risks, and act based on what I knew. As I contemplated retooling my practice, I shifted into data-gathering mode. Early within the process, I began to meet Ruby developers to understand what was so special about Ruby. Then, I talked to managers. I wanted to understand who was using Ruby for production applications and how hard they were willing to push it. I talked to skeptics to understand where they thought the biggest holes might be. Next, I tried Ruby on Rails on something beyond trivial. It fell short of my expectations in some ways but far surpassed them in most others. Now, I'm working on strategies to integrate Java with Ruby. I'll start doing integration projects in the near future. In this book, you'll learn what I've learned. I'll tell you how far and hard I think you can push Ruby. I'm excited about the language, and I'll try to tell you about Java's limitations, where Ruby is an appropriate choice. I will also warn you where Java may be a better choice, or Ruby is not quite mature.

Be forewarned, though. This field is moving rapidly and will doubtless change many times in the next few years.

In this chapter, we'll look at the emergence of new technologies, especially programming languages. Then, we'll look broadly at a process you can use to decide whether to take the plunge. Finally, we'll see what some Ruby visionaries have to say about moving from Java to Ruby.

1.2 The Java Platform Is Weakening

Successful programming languages seem to emerge every decade or so. Bell Labs developed the C programming language in the early 1970s, and C emerged in the mid-1970s as a commercially successful language for applications. The new language had critical advantages that application languages of the time didn't have: speed and close affinity with the rapidly emerging Unix operating system. C++ was released by AT&T in 1985 and slowly subsumed C because it had features allowing object-oriented programming. Sun released Java in 1996, and it rapidly emerged as a popular language for Internet development. Java has been growing steadily ever since.

Figure 1.1, on the facing page, shows the overall timeline, with a new language emerging every decade or so.[1] FORTRAN in the early 1950s and COBOL in the early 1960s reinforce this trend. If you believe the trend will continue, we're due for a new programming language around now, and Java should start to decline soon. If you pay careful attention to the trade press, you're probably already seeing some signs of decline:

- *Complexity.* Java's complexity is increasing. With one massively complex framework after another, Java vendors embraced EJB and the most complicated version imaginable of web services and XML. EJB vendors redesigned EJB from scratch twice, forcing significant migrations on their customers.

---

[1]http://www.levenez.com/lang/history.html

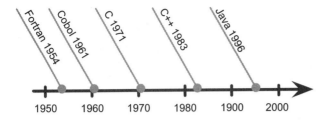

Figure 1.1: LANGUAGE TIMELINE

- *Availability.* In a 2003 study, Wily reported that J2EE performance and availability were generally average to poor. To add fuel to the fire, Java Lobby, a Java evangelist organization, published an article called "The Fabled 'Five Eights' of J2EE Availability." This term stuck and has been hotly debated ever since.[2]

- *Competition.* In February 2005, IBM announced consulting support for PHP. Ruby on Rails has passed 500,000 total downloads. By the middle of 2006, there will be seven books about Ruby on Rails. Peter Yared, Sun's previous application server CTO, predicted that J2EE would lose to LAMP (open source software consisting of Linux, Apache web server, MySQL, and a dynamic language such as Python, Perl, or PHP).[3]

Still, most executives embrace Java or the Microsoft equivalent, .NET. Alternatives may as well not even exist. We've created an environment where the popular decisions are safe, even if the popular decision is wrong. But I believe Ruby will emerge soon. Many of Java's visionaries—including James Duncan Davidson, the creator of two of the most successful Java open source projects of all time—are betting on Ruby on Rails. Let's quickly look at how new technologies, including programming languages, emerge.

1.3 Early Adopters Embrace Ruby

In *Crossing the Chasm* [Moo99], Geoffrey Moore presents a theory about the adoption of technology. Figure 1.2, on the next page shows his tech-

---

[2]http://www.wilytech.com/news/releases/031120.html
[3]http://www.theserverside.com/news/thread.tss?thread_id=36129

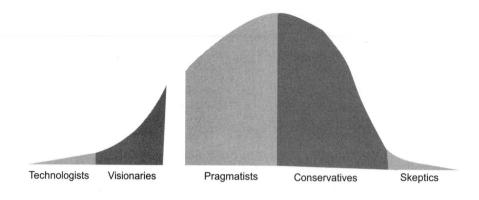

Technologists Visionaries Pragmatists Conservatives Skeptics

Figure 1.2: TECHNOLOGY ADOPTION CURVE

nology adoption graph. The X axis represents time, and the Y axis represents market share. Moore believes that technology adoption comes in five groups. Technology enthusiasts will play with technology because it's fun and informative. Visionaries come next, applying technology to achieve competitive advantage when they see big rewards that offset high risks. These two groups together are early adopters. Later, the mass market follows with pragmatists and conservatives in a huge wave of adoption. Skeptics trickle in last. Moore argues that many unsuccessful technologies stall after the visionaries adopt the technology because pragmatists look for safe choices, and that's the rub for new technologies. A new language must show it can "cross the chasm" to be commercially successful, but the mass market will not adopt a new language until it has crossed the chasm.

With new programming languages, the chasm is a massive obstacle. The problem for new adopters is daunting: to get the biggest competitive advantage, you must be willing to bet that a new language will be enticing to risk-averse pragmatists, but without an established community that makes the technology safe, a new language will rarely be enticing enough. In *Beyond Java* [Tat05], I argue that the chasm for new languages is bigger than the chasm for many other new technologies because of the need for a supporting community. A language needs community to supply enough education, enhancements, programmers, and aftermarket extensions to make the language worthwhile. So, new languages rarely grow slowly to prominence. Instead, either they explode or they stall and never enter the mainstream. With explosive growth, the chasm becomes much less of an issue, because pragmatists can see evidence of rapid growth and the promise of community for the new technology, so the risk becomes much smaller.

Ruby is exploding today, and the catalyst is productivity, thanks to a framework called Ruby on Rails. The intended niche for Ruby on Rails is database-backed Internet applications. This is clearly the most important application niche, and we'll focus on this space within this book; however, I'm convinced that the benefits of Ruby reach far beyond any single framework, and you'll see many examples within this book of people who have used Ruby without Rails and achieved impressive productivity. In today's marketplace, productivity is king. Some interesting innovations in Ruby on Rails make it several times more productive than Java for an important class of applications. Some features of Ruby make it more productive than Java as an application or scripting language.

You may be reading this book right now because you've heard about some of those great productivity numbers and because you can't afford to ignore them. You're right. I'm not going to belittle the enormous risk of adopting a new programming language, but let's look at how Ruby early adopters tend to mitigate that risk.

Risk

In this book, the central question is this: how can you justify the massive risk of moving to a new programming language? I won't pretend to make this decision for you, but I will show you how I came to this decision for my practice, and I'll walk you through what others have done. My intuition tells me Java development is getting riskier as Ruby development gets safer. Although my metrics may be disputable, I do have eight years of experience working with Java customers, and I have close relationships to Java visionaries who are observing the same phenomenon.

As the risks for Java increase, Ruby's risks will diminish as its market share rises. Eventually, these trend lines will surely cross, at least for certain problem sets as shown in Figure 1.3, on the following page. You'll have to measure the risk of stagnation of a new programming language, leading to spectacular injury, against the greater risk of highly probable death by a thousand pin pricks—bugs, cost overruns, and delays.

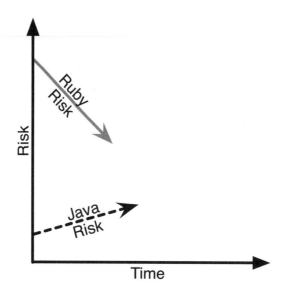

Figure 1.3: JAVA'S RISKS ARE INCREASING OVER TIME

Those who make the Ruby decision early will have a tremendous advantage over those who have to wait. That's what's driving the investment of dozens of Java visionaries, and that's what's fueling Ruby's explosion.

I won't dwell too long on why I believe Ruby will emerge just yet. Instead, let's look at how you might decide to move to Ruby, and how you might act on that decision.

1.4 The Process

The structure of this book is based on the phases, shown in Figure 1.4, on the next page, that you might go through as you introduce a new language. Each chapter in the book will walk you through part of that flowchart. You can see the three distinct phases of the decision:

- *Gather information.* In this phase, you seek to understand your own Java-based pain and what you expect to gain from a new programming language. Pain, potential risk, and potential reward are all part of this equation.

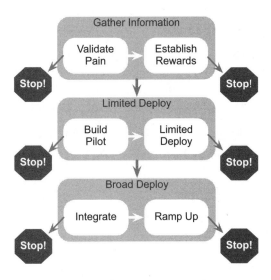

Figure 1.4: RUBY ADOPTION DECISION CHART

- *Limited deployment.* In this phase, you try Ruby in a pilot, and if it is successful, you deploy that pilot. You may then begin to take on limited, isolated projects with Ruby. At this point, risks are relatively low, based on the limited deployment.

- *Broad deployment.* In this phase, you expand the scope of your Ruby deployments. This set of risks is much different from working with limited deployments. You'll need strategies for your integration with other applications, and you'll also need to understand how you'll go about recruiting talent.

Validating Pain

The first step in any significant technical transition is evaluating the need. The most expensive migration is one that never should have happened. If you're one of Moore's technologists or visionaries, you might be tempted to plunge headlong into Ruby, without assessing your pain, but it is better to take the time to understand what Java's limitations are costing you. A cost assessment in your back pocket can be an excellent insurance policy against trouble.

Establishing Rewards

With the costs of Java development firmly in your pocket, your next move is to understand the benefits of Ruby. For this step, you'll try to make as direct a comparison between Java and Ruby as you can. You'll use tangible and intangible evidence to support your thought process:

- *Costs.* You'll directly compare your cost structure under Java to a similar one for Ruby. You'll take into account both hard and soft costs.

- *Visionary opinions.* The opinions of several people in the industry carry more weight than others. The movement of visionaries to Ruby or away from Java could also lend support to a Ruby decision.

- *Team dynamics.* This intangible factor will become increasingly important as Ruby continues to emerge. If the emergence of Ruby is like that of other languages, you'll find developers want to use it because it's a new and marketable skill.

- *Maintenance.* There aren't any empirical studies about the cost of maintaining Java versus alternatives, but some circumstantial evidence suggests that maintaining simpler systems costs much less, and other studies suggest that applications with fewer lines of code are generally easier to maintain.

The Pilot

If you've established that Ruby is in your future, the next step is to establish some success with working code. You can choose from many strategies to help you do so:

- A conservative team can build a prototype in Ruby that's representative of a real-world application. You can show a shorter cycle time or a richer application or both.

- A consulting team can start a Ruby project, at its own expense, in parallel with a Java project. When the customer is convinced of the benefits (such as lower cost or richer features), the Java version can be disbanded.

- A team with a variety of old and new projects can choose a small, low-risk internal application in Ruby instead of Java. Most companies have inwardly facing applications that might not be mission critical. The best pilot projects have high visibility and low risk.

- An aggressive team can build the same high-risk application in parallel, once in Ruby and once in Java. Usually, the Ruby team will be much smaller. As the Ruby team demonstrates competence, the Java effort can be disbanded.

The best options usually deliver tangible business value quickly. We'll go over each of these scenarios and back them up with people who have implemented successful pilots with each technique.

Picking Technologies

After you've established success, you'll want to take stock of Ruby and its world. Once you've gotten a good handle on it, you'll want to compare Ruby technologies to Java technologies at a very high level to get your head around what a particular migration will require.

You don't need a whole lot of deep technical detail. You just need a high-level understanding of the tools at your disposal. You'll want to understand the Ruby language, how you'll handle issues such as persistence or security, and web development strategies. In short, you'll want to know what Ruby can do for you.

Integrating the Old World

If you have much invested in Java code, you won't be able to migrate overnight, and you shouldn't try. Many companies run Java, COBOL, and C++ side by side quite effectively. The key to understanding your overall migration plan is knowing the integration strategies available to you.

We'll highlight these strategies:

- You can integrate coarsely. Using this strategy, you make major chunks of your Java applications available remotely, usually over some Internet standards. Web services and service-oriented architectures are two examples of this approach.

- You can use web services or prepackaged middleware. Messaging software (such as IBM's MQ or BEA's Business Integration Suite) usually provides good C APIs that Ruby can use.

- You can use fine-grained integration. Using this strategy, you use special software to let Java and Ruby talk together at very low levels. You'll see several frameworks that use this approach.

When you have a clear strategy for how you want your Java and Ruby applications to interoperate, you stand a much better chance of success. Big bangs—migrations that must happen all at once—are rarely successful. A good integration strategy goes a long way toward helping you deliver business value throughout your transition, and that means greater success.

Ramping Up

Once you know how your system will fit together, it's time to ramp up your development effort. You might be surprised to know how much harder it will be to find Ruby developers over the short run. Don't let that deter you. You can often teach a Java developer Ruby faster than you can teach her many Java frameworks. We'll look at strategies to find and hire Ruby developers.

Weighing Scope and Risk

Once you have an idea of your potential gains, it's time to focus on the other side of the equation. As an emerging programming language, Ruby has a different set of challenges from Java:

- As a new language, Ruby could potentially stagnate, which could make scarce resources even harder to find.

- There are not as many deployed Ruby applications in production yet, so we don't have as much definitive proof of the ultimate scalability of Ruby.

- The Ruby community is not as well established as the Java community, so it's harder to find third-party components, frameworks, education, and services.

- Ruby is less structured than Java and has fewer automated features to protect applications from abuse. This flexibility is both a strength and a weakness.

To be fair, many Java developers face the same set of risks on a smaller scale. The number of Java frameworks is exploding, with dozens of new open source and commercial frameworks emerging monthly. But Ruby is especially vulnerable to these risks, so you have got to take them seriously and carefully weigh them against the potential benefits.

1.5 Moving Ahead

Ruby is real. Java visionaries I know are moving aggressively toward it, investing by creating education, writing books, and generally paving the way for the masses to follow. Education companies are ramping up to offer courses on Ruby on Rails. In the chapters that follow, you'll see what has Java visionaries concerned and Ruby visionaries enthused. You'll also see the deep questions that all of us must answer as we move from Java to Ruby.

1.6 Executive Summary

- Java is bogging down under too many frameworks.

- The integrated Rails environment counters this complexity.

- Early Rails adoption is very strong.

- Moving to Ruby involves gathering information, establishing an early limited pilot, and deploying more broadly.

- Risk is inevitable, but Java's risks are understated.

We must all suffer one of two things: the pain of discipline or the pain of regret or disappointment.
  ► Jim Rohn

Chapter 2

Pain

If you want to truly know the health of your project, you have to get in touch with your pain. Athletes need to strike a balance between nagging twinges and deeper telling aches; development managers must distinguish between mere hiccups and symptoms of damaging disease. If you're succeeding with Java with only nagging pain—if you're delivering software your customers want on time within your budget and with happy developers—you probably shouldn't consider moving to Ruby. But if your aches run deep and are the symptoms of real disease, you have to act. The first step of introducing any new technology must be recognizing pain.

2.1 The House of Pain

After hearing all the hype around Ruby on Rails and other frameworks, you might be tempted to bolt for the exit too soon, but take a deep breath first. Don't let anyone tell you that Ruby is the answer to every question. Java does have some tremendous advantages over most other programming languages:

- *Java's population of programmers is huge.* With Java's massive pool of programmers, you can always find developers to hire or supplement your staff with temps, consultants, or even offshore development.

- *Java's open source community thrives.* Open source projects exist across a wide spectrum of problem spaces and fill many different niches. With Java, you can often get software for free that you'd have to build yourself or pay for on other languages.

- *Java is mature.* Java is often the safest choice.

- *Java is scalable.* We've learned enough from experience to build applications that scale.

- *Java offers choice.* You don't have to paint yourself into a corner with Java, because you have so many open standards defining many important interfaces and vendors to choose from.

Technology

In general, Java is a safe choice. It's mature, complete, and ready for outsourcing. For good reasons, Java has dominated Internet integration projects. Sure, Java can handle the most difficult enterprise integration issues. It has got features to solve notoriously hard problems:

- *Two-phase commit.* When the same application needs to coordinate two resources—such as two databases, for example—you sometimes need sophisticated software to tie the two together to keep things consistent. That software often uses two-phase commit, and Java supports it.

- *Powerful object-relational mapping.* Say your company's new DBA, a PhD student with ten years of schooling but no practical experience, proudly brings you a database model that is in 14th normal form. After they stop screaming, your programmers tell you they have never heard of 14th normal form, but they are quite sure that they don't want to subject their object model to such torture.

  Instead, your best programmers use a framework to translate data between the database schema and the objects of your application. That technique is known as object-relational mapping. Java has mature frameworks that do it well; Ruby doesn't.

- *Distributed objects.* When you need to build applications that span many different computers across the room, or even across the ocean, you sometimes need specialized software to help different pieces of the application communicate. Java can manage distributed objects in many ways. Ruby's options are more limited.

Ruby does have some simple transaction management and some rudimentary object-relational mapping, but those frameworks are nowhere near as powerful or as proven as their Java counterparts. If you were to attack any of these problems with Ruby today, you'd possibly wind up writing too much infrastructure and glue code.

With Java, a whole lot of your glue code comes for free. Treat these enterprise problems as if they were elephants. You can't bring down an elephant with a toothpick or a Swiss army knife. You need an elephant gun. The Java platform is an elephant gun.

The Hierarchy of Pain

I once talked to a customer about the problems in her enterprise. After questioning her developers and reading code, I strongly suspected that productivity was her biggest problem. In fact, I was wrong. They were horribly unproductive, but given the business climate, it didn't matter. Their group was dependent on requirements from three different business units, and the development team frequently had to wait weeks at a time for new requirements. It dawned on me that the director was telling me the truth. *Java development was simply not a bottleneck.* If Java is not the problem, don't go looking for a solution.

To be successful, you need to understand the pain in your organization and interpret it. You need to know where the pain is the most acute. Most projects don't fail for technical reasons. If you can't solve your communication problems, if you can't control scope creep, or if you can't tell what the customer actually wants, the choice of programming language is not going to matter to you. It's simply not high enough in the hierarchy of pain. Put this book down, and pick up another one. Ruby won't help; it will only introduce more risk.

But if you're inclined to believe that a simpler, more productive language would help, read on. Too many people worship Java, and too many vendors tell you you that Java can be all things to all people, and therein lies another kind of risk. Using the wrong tool for the job, even when it's the most popular tool, costs you money. Many of the problems that we solve with Java simply aren't elephants. I'd argue the problem we solve *most often* with Java—putting a web-based user interface on a relational database—isn't an elephant. It's a fuzzy little bunny rabbit. Or a squirrel. Although you can probably kill a rabbit with an elephant gun, bad things usually happen when you do.

Solve the wrong problem with the wrong technology, and the real pain begins. When Java was invented, it was simple, nimble, and robust when compared to most alternatives. But the pain crept up on us, slowly building from an itch to a piercing, throbbing crescendo. Let's look at the types of problems you're likely to find with the Java platform.

2.2 Poor Productivity

More than any other characteristic of any programming language, you can translate productivity to bottom-line dollars. Let each worker do more, and you can carry less staff. Work faster, and your application can deliver value to the business sooner. In most cases, productivity is *the most important consideration* for software development. Whether your project emphasizes quality, features, availability, or performance, productivity is the key to get you there. The best development teams build software in three stages:

- Make it work (delivery).
- Make it right (quality).
- Make it fast (performance).

You can't attack quality or performance without first getting your base running. And you certainly need to make an application available before you can make it highly available. It's all about evolution. You need to deliver tangible business value with every step. In this industry, we've learned that the most productive software development happens in smaller iterations. You simply can't be productive by building fast, clean applications with all possible features the first pass through your development cycle. You'll drown in the details, and you'll likely throw too much code away. It's far better to get something running and then improve it quickly.

You may be using Java because you think it's a clean language and it will save you time in the long run by improving your productivity over the long haul. You are betting that you can introduce new features faster, introduce fewer bugs, and fix the ones that sneak in more quickly.

Why Is Productivity So Important?

Here's an example from another industry. When Japan started building cars, they didn't build them very well. In fact, Japan had a reputation for building junk. They needed to improve quality, and the best path to do so was one iteration at a time.

Japan's quality improved after they applied the technique of Statistical Process Control (SPC) to their manufacturing. The inventor of SPC, Edward Walter Demming, tried to get the United States to adopt these methods in post–World War II America, and it didn't take hold; so,

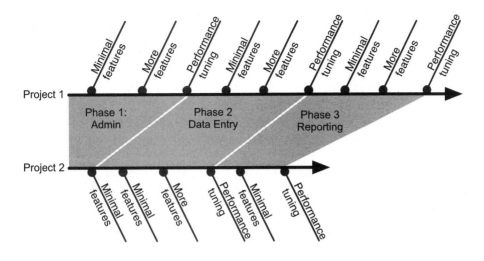

Figure 2.1: PROJECT 1'S TEAM CONCENTRATED ON UNNECESSARY DETAIL TOO SOON

he took it to Japan, where they needed to rebuild their manufacturing infrastructure after the war. Demming was treated like a god in Japan. They applied his SPC techniques religiously in their automotive industry and eventually unseated Detroit as the top-selling auto manufacturer. They improved slowly, focusing on improving process, especially their cycle time between generations. With a shorter cycle time and leadership focused on process improvement, Tokyo's cars improved faster than Detroit's.

You can apply the same principle to software. With better productivity, you have more time to focus on improvements to features, performance, and quality, *based on the needs of the business*. Figure 2.1 shows the story. If you had three major pieces of an application to deliver (admin, data entry, and reporting) and you focused on building fast, perfect, feature-rich software for each major component, it would take you a certain amount of time—arbitrarily call it 15 units, if nothing went wrong.

If instead you put something in front of your customers after satisfying your initial set of requirements, you'd learn things from your customers that could save you time. Let's say that each initial iteration takes one unit of time. Assume your administrators say that the new admin console is fine; in fact, it's far better than the one they're using. Still, you know of some bugs to fix, so you allocate one unit of time for polishing work. Now, let's say your analysts do not like the reporting feature, finding it crude, limiting, and slow (four units). You'd need to do some rework, combined with some polishing and performance work. Customer service reps liked the look and feel of the system, but it could not keep up with the call volume. You'd have to improve performance (two units). You have delivered your software in less than half the time.

So, your goal isn't to be perfect right out of the gate—your goal is to get out of the gate quickly. Then, you iteratively improve. The quicker your iterations, the better off you are. With most applications, rather than anticipating the needs of your users, you should instead strive to get code in front of your users quickly. Then, based on their feedback and the needs of your business, you can apply your resources to address performance optimization, features, and other improvements. Take a lesson from Japan. Strive to cycle faster, and improve with each iteration. If you can do both, you'll beat your competition. That's true in manufacturing, and that's true in software.

Productivity of Core Java

In terms of productivity, in order to understand how Java comes up short, you have to know where it came from. In 1996, C++ was the dominant programming language for application development on server platforms. C++ was not a very productive language, but it *was* fast. At the time, we thought speed was more important than productivity. C++ had all the marketing momentum (from all the Unix vendors, Microsoft, and IBM, among others). C++ had the community. But when conditions are right, new programming languages emerge and old ones fade.

Any new programming language needs a catalyst to get the community rolling. Programming languages need a community in order to achieve widespread success, but it's hard to get new users without a community. When Sun created Java and embedded it into the Netscape Navigator Internet browser, they made some excellent compromises to ramp up a Java community in a hurry:

- Sun made Java look like C++. Java adopted a syntax like that of C++. With a C++-like language, Java didn't have to establish its own community from scratch. It could simply lure in C++ developers.

- Sun made Java act like C++ in a few important ways. Object-oriented languages let you build applications with a certain kind of building block: an object. Objects have both behavior and data, rolled up together. C++ cheats on object orientation, because some C++ elements, like characters and numbers, are not really objects. Java cheats in the same way.

- Sun copied a C++ feature called *static typing*. Static typing means that certain pieces of an application have one type, and you have to declare that type in advance. Many of the most productive languages for building applications use a different strategy, called *dynamic typing*.

In *Beyond Java*, I assert that Java's creators had to make these compromises to succeed. But compromises have two sides. By building a language that was closer to C++ than alternatives such as Smalltalk or Lisp, Sun was able to attract C++ users to the fledgling language. The downside of these compromises is productivity. C, and C++ by extension, was never designed to build applications. It was designed to build operating systems such as Unix. C++ was designed to be flexible and to produce fast systems code, not to productively build applications. We're now paying for the compromises:

- The C++ syntax, combined with Java's static typing, means programmers have to type too much—Java programs have two to four times the number of characters of similar programs in more dynamic languages such as Ruby. Many believe that shorter programs reduce maintenance costs proportionately.

- Java's static typing requires a compiler, so the compiler can check certain details for programmers, such as several forms of compatibility between two parts of a program. As a consequence, Java developers have to go through an extra compile step hundreds of times a day. Ruby developers don't.

- Java's primitives, are not object-oriented; this means that Java libraries must often be many times larger than libraries for purely object-oriented languages. For example, object-oriented languages have features to turn objects into XML. Similar Java programs have to deal with objects, but also characters, numbers, Booleans, and several other primitive types.

The available evidence to support programmer productivity for any language is remarkably scarce. One of the most compelling studies I've

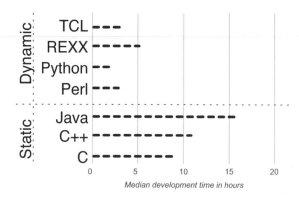

Figure 2.2: THE PRODUCTIVITY OF SEVEN DIFFERENT LANGUAGES

seen on the topic is very old and does not relate directly to Ruby. I mention it here only because every single dynamically typed language, the so-called scripting languages, did much better than its statically typed peers. Figure 2.2 shows the results of a report[1] comparing productivity of dynamic languages such as Python, REXX, and Tcl to static languages such as C++ and Java. Surprisingly, Java is the worst language in the study, being around one third as productive as the scripting alternatives. Further, Java programs were generally two to three times as long as programs from the scripting languages. You could argue that tools and frameworks have gotten better since then, but we've also seen extensive bloating and a proliferation of frameworks. To many, these problems represent a productivity gash too large for any IDE to patch.

In Chapter 4, *Pilot*, on page 61, we'll look at a number of reasons that Ruby development can be many times as productive as Java development for certain problem domains. If you're interested but not convinced, you can do a prototype and measure productivity for yourself.

Productivity in Frameworks

You might think you could sacrifice some productivity when you're dealing with the low-level Java programming language and make up that time by using one of the thousands of Java frameworks. Usually, you'd be wrong.

---

[1]http://page.mi.fu-berlin.de/~prechelt/Biblio/jccpprt_computer2000.pdf

Essential complexity is the complexity required to do a job. If your application does tax returns, your application is going to be at least as complex as the requirements in the tax law. *Nonessential complexity*, also called *accidental complexity*, deals with the complexity you introduce to your environment. Martin Fowler, one of the most influential consultants in the computing profession, suggests Java frameworks introduce too much nonessential complexity. When you look at the history of enterprise computing in Java, you have to conclude he's right.

What's wrong with Java?—A discussion with Martin Fowler

Chief scientist of ThoughtWorks,
author of Patterns of Enterprise Application Architecture

Q: What was your first object-oriented programming language?

Early in my career, I had an interest in objects. I worked with Smalltalk and C++. Most people at that time started with one or the other, but knowing both gave me a certain advantage. I got a distinctly schizophrenic view of the world. I was always conscious of the benefits of Smalltalk over C++. I didn't believe that people should use C++ for enterprise applications, but they did. When Java came along, we gained some, primarily because Java killed C++ for enterprise application development. But like many old Smalltalkers, I felt Java was a step backward from Smalltalk.

Q: What are the advantages of Java over Ruby?

With Java, you get sophisticated tools. I feel the pain when I have to leave the Intellij IDE. For companies, the stability of Java (and .NET, Java's separated-at-birth twin) is important, because post-COBOL, things were unstable with many languages and tools where it was hard to see what would last.

Q: What are the limitations of Java as you see them?

I usually hear people complain about static typing, which is important but not the whole story. Java guys spend too much time dealing with all the technical stuff that surrounds the core business behavior; this is complexity that's not helping to deal with the business problem. Our CEO (ThoughtWorks CEO Roy Singham) likes to taunt Java by saying it has failed the enterprise. The fact that we have to do all of this machinery means developers are not thinking enough about business issues. They're thinking about how to move data in and out of a database, and in and out of a GUI.

Q: Where did Java go wrong?

There's so much of a push in the Java world to keep lesser-skilled developers from making messes, and that idea has failed. The idea that you can keep people from shooting themselves in the foot is appealing, but it's not what we've seen in practice. There are far too many overly complex bad Java apps out there.

Overall, Java is just too complicated. *No Silver Bullet* (Bro86) made the distinction between essential and accidental complexity. For example, if you're building a payroll system, the payroll business rules represent real complexity. But with Java, accidental complexity is most of the total effort. The EJB fiasco made this worse. EJB is a stunningly complex framework but is far too complex for most of the applications we see. Spring and Hibernate are a huge step forward, but there's still this nagging feeling that there's too much accidental complexity.

Q: Do you see any real alternatives to Java?

In the enterprise space in the last six years, a dark horse is stalking the .NET/Java duopoly: LAMP. LAMP stands for Linux, Apache, MySQL, and one of the *P-scripting* languages from PHP, Perl, and Python. In reality, LAMP has come to signify some combination of open source frameworks, plus a scripting language. By that definition, Ruby is an honorary part of the LAMP equation; you just have to ignore the downstroke on the *R*.

I used Perl for a little while, but I gave up when I couldn't even read some of the stuff I wrote. Some things in LAMP are now getting more interesting because the scripting languages are getting closer—application designs are getting better. I got into Python for a while, because objects were much more fluent, and it was much more dynamic than Java.

But don't forget that these are still early days. As I talk about this, we don't have much experience of Rails in the field.

At the moment it looks good, good enough to be worth exploring further, but until we see the practice in the field, we won't know for sure.

Q: Can Java be fixed?

That's an interesting question. You need to first answer the question, "What do they need to do to evolve the language to look more like the languages that feel more comfortable?" I'm not completely sure what that list is, but we could come up with such a list. But it's not just the language. It's all of the libraries. Can you meld those to take advantage of the new languages? What impact will new language fixes have on the frameworks? Are the frameworks going to be able to become more dynamic? Or are there so many frameworks that we've become locked into a static mind-set?

On another level, can people really replicate the design decisions that David Heinemeier Hansson (creator of Ruby on Rails) made? Take convention over configuration. It's one of those things where people can worry about all of the things that can go wrong instead of concentrating on what's going right. I like that decision. It's gutsy and so much against conventional wisdom. Lots of evidence suggests that it does work. Can that decision be brought into Java frameworks?

Q: Will Java be fixed?

I don't really care. Because one way or another, we win. My heart is behind the underdog, though.

EJB

Since about 1999, most of the commercial Java brainpower has been focused on the hardest enterprise problems. In December 1998, the Java Community Process (JCP), unleashed the EJB (Enterprise JavaBeans) framework onto the Java developer population.

This terrible creature was very powerful, but that beast brought along too many of its own problems, including unmanageable complexity and poor performance.

Most experts now agree that early versions of EJB were unmitigated disasters. Since 1999, EJB experts have scrapped and rewritten big pieces of EJB specification *twice.*

Many authors are now critical of the EJB albatross. My book *Bitter EJB* [Tat03] concentrated on the problems with EJB entity beans (the standard for letting EJB code access databases). The Internet has hundreds of sites chronicling problems with EJB. EJB has gotten a little better, but it's still an albatross, and the big vendors supporting it refuse to give up. EJB is an elephant cannon of the highest order, yet most EJB developers that I know use it to build objects, backed by relational databases, with a web-based user interface on top. At best, EJB is a niche solution for problems requiring advanced capabilities such as distributed transactions.

XML

Java is pretty good at specifying behavior and data types, but doesn't express data itself very well. Enter XML (eXtensible Markup Language). XML offers Java programmers a way to structure data better so their programs can interpret that data better. Java developers embraced XML the same way they embraced EJB.

XML is a markup language based on an older document language called SGML. Early versions were relatively simple, but new versions seem to have solved that problem. XML designers have added features called Schema and Namespaces, making XML a little easier for the toughest problems but much more cumbersome for everything else. Like EJB, XML has become overkill for many of the problems Java developers most need to solve.

XML has now crept so far into the collective psyche of Java developers that the line between Java development and XML development is getting harder and harder to draw. Java developers use XML to define configuration, specify business rules, describe documents and messages, write programs, and even name their kids. And Java is a worse language for it.

Microsoft and IBM now hype up web services with the same energy and fervor once reserved for EJB. Web services are used to invoke programs remotely, over the Web. It's a noble idea, but the web services designers seem to be making many of the same mistakes that EJB and XML creators did. Rather than focus on making it easy for simple Java applications to communicate on the Internet, they increasingly seek to solve the most difficult problems for enterprise uber-programmers, at the expense of the masses of everyday programmers who could easily make a simpler solution work.

In Tim O'Reilly's talk "What Is Web 2.0"[2] he describes the adoption of web services at Amazon.com. At the peak of the web services craze, Amazon.com had a set of remote services they wanted to make available. They provided two versions of their API. The first was web services. With all the hype surrounding web services, it's not surprising that most Amazon.com clients tried the web services version first. But Amazon made another version of their API available, using a simpler services API called ReST (Representational State Transfer). Surprisingly, over time, 95% of Amazon.com clients moved from the web services API to the ReST-based API, because the newer API is simpler, cleaner and generally more productive. Web services remind me of my best friend's Jaguar: the performance is nice on paper, but the car is always in the shop.

It should come as no surprise to you that Java vendors heavily back web services, EJB, and XML. Java frameworks look oddly impressive, but the Java community has not yet learned to build truly productive frameworks. In fact, we don't even know what to measure. Analysts such as Gartner write reports[3] showing productivity *gains of Java over C++*. If your goal is to boost productivity, C++ should not be your goal! We should compare productivity in Java with languages built to write applications, not systems software.

As the current versions of Struts, EJB and web services fade, giving way to lightweight versions, many open source frameworks are striving to fill the open spaces. As they do, the explosion of open source frameworks, combined with new commercial APIs, leads to another significant source of pain: confusion. Making the right choice is a difficult and exhausting process. Guessing wrong can doom a project to failure or paralyzing bloat. The proliferation of APIs is not a unique problem. It's a response to a complicated language with a complicated set of frameworks. The Java developer can do nothing but try to cope.

---

[2]http://www.oreillynet.com/pub/a/oreilly/tim/news/2005/09/30/what-is-web-20.html

[3]http://www.javaworld.com/javaworld/jw-02-2001/jw-0209-itw-javajobs.html

2.3 Long Ramp-Up

If long-term productivity is a problem for Java, short-term productivity is a disaster. For me, teaching Java used to be pure joy. Now, it's incredibly tedious. In 2003, I wrote *Better, Faster, Lighter Java* [Tat04]. In it, I talked about a set of principles for lightweight development. I then suggested a combination of simplified open source technologies that a developer could use to solve simple problems:

- *An MVC framework.* A web-based framework such as Struts separates the model, view and controller. Most developers recognize that options such as Tapestry and JSF (JavaServer Faces) are emerging, but Struts is by far the most popular Java MVC framework.

- *The Spring framework.* The Spring framework provides the glue code necessary to wire together system services with application logic.

- *Hibernate.* Java development usually calls for *persistence*, or saving Java objects to a database. Hibernate lets developers access relational databases through ordinary Java objects.

Each of these sophisticated technologies allows good programmers to build better code in less time than conventional Java frameworks, but there's a cost: they're complex. Each of these technologies has at least one 600-page book written about it, and most of them have several books that are even longer. You can find courses that teach either Spring or Hibernate *for several weeks.* These frameworks make sense when you're building heavy-duty enterprise applications, but for most web-based development, they are overkill. Keep in mind that we're talking about the frameworks touted as the *simple* Java solutions. The result is that Java is no longer as approachable as it once was—you have to learn too much to get started.

In August 2005, I spent a week with a customer, training some new Java developers to build lightweight applications. Eventually, it was time to lay out the education plan for the customer. I presented five courses: basic Java, web-based programming with Tapestry, enterprise development with Spring, database access with Hibernate, and a class on their development tools. I could see the drooping body language of the potential students as I worked my way down the list. With each topic, their shoulders slumped a little more under the weight of the new requirements.

Course	Description	Duration
Web-based Java	Basic Java and servlets	1 week
Hibernate	Database access with Hibernate	1 week
Agile development tools	IDEA, JUnit, CVS, Ant and CruiseControl	2 weeks
Tapestry	Web-based user interfaces	1 week

Figure 2.3: EXAMPLE SYLLABUS FOR LIGHTWEIGHT DEVELOPMENT

Here's the kicker. The manager asked whether his team would be able to build an application without help. I had to say "Absolutely not." Sure, they could write a supercharged version of the first traditional Java application, a web and database-enabled "Hello, World," but they wouldn't have any experience. They would need some time to make some mistakes. To even recognize those mistakes, they'd need mentors looking over their shoulders. The brutal truth was plain—to join even the lightweight Java club, they'd have to pay a high initiation fee and learn many secret handshakes. Joining the club would take much more time than they wanted to invest.

Even Java developers with experience are not immune to steep learning curves. A developer with good experience with JDBC, Java's most basic database access API (application programming interface), would still have to work hard and long to learn alternative persistence frameworks such as Hibernate or JDO. Frameworks that provide the glue code to hold applications together, like EJB (Enterprise JavaBeans) and Spring, might make a developer more productive, but they also add to the learning curve. Throw in presentation frameworks, and the workload becomes oppressive.

If either your team or a potential new hire does not have good Java experience, expect at least a month and a half of course work and another three to six months of development time to achieve modest productivity. For lead developers or architects, ramping up will take longer. In the best conditions, it will take a Java developer two to five years to learn enough of a stack of enterprise frameworks to lead a team or project.

2.4 A Look at Risk

You've probably heard the old cliché: no one has ever been fired for choosing IBM. As long as any monopoly reigns, the safest choice is usually the wisest one. But after several years of stagnation, Java may be the most *popular* choice, but it's no longer always the *safest* choice. In a global economy, bad choices, even popular ones, can burn you badly.

Outsourcing

Offshoring centers like the ones in Bangalore, India, have tens of thousands of developers providing an inexpensive programming alternative. Make no mistake; in many cases, these centers have programmers who are motivated, skilled, and talented. If your development organization doesn't communicate with your customers, it doesn't matter whether they're in the next building, the next state, or overseas. India's outsourcing shops increasingly have presences in major United States and European markets with improving project management.

But with unproductive programming languages, communicating with your customer is much more difficult. If it takes you too long between a customer request and showing them results on the screen, your customer will lose interest.

If you're not productive, you're not cost-effective, and your project is vulnerable. Outsourcing operations are finding more and more innovative ways to work with corporations abroad. But we're finding that certain types of projects do not lend themselves to outsourcing. If you want to keep your job safe, your projects need features that offshoring cannot easily replicate:

- *Productivity.* Outsourcing takes much more management overhead. A colleague who outsources his programming says he has to pay developers about 30% of what he pays developers in Raleigh, North Carolina. The catch is that he has to be much more diligent with his project management. With the extra project management overhead, he pays 70 cents for every dollar he'd pay local programmers. So if you can reduce your costs by just 30%, you can often improve your chances.

- *Communication.* If you're communicating with your customers several times a week and if the communication is productive, you're using your biggest advantage over offshoring centers: proximity.

The ocean between you and them got smaller with the invention of the Internet, but overseas programmers aren't there to look your customer in the eye and read her facial expression when you show her that new demo. Offshore operations have a culture and language barrier to overcome. You don't. But Java's productivity won't let you put new features in front of your customer nearly often enough, so Java projects are at risk for outsourcing.

- *New technologies.* Outsourcing centers won't want to use leading-edge technologies. They will want to use technologies that are broadly used and more mature. Ruby will be safer from outsourcing shops until it's a mainstream technology.

Competition

In *Beyond Java*, I make the case that key Java visionaries know that Java is fading. As the programming industry wakes up, we're going to recognize that Java is not the best possible fit for a wide spectrum of applications. Consider once again the most common programming problem: capturing and manipulating relational database data from a web-based user interface. The newer technologies, such as Ruby on Rails, will be disruptive. Most consultants I know believe that Ruby on Rails is several *times* as productive as similar Java frameworks. Usually, a productivity edge of a couple of percentage points is enormous. When you consider the huge productivity reports of two to ten times attributed to Ruby, they're even bigger.

But you can't limit Ruby's productivity to a single aspect of development. Consider one of Ruby's primary strengths: metaprogramming. This language feature lets Ruby programmers extend Ruby painlessly. When you metaprogram, you write programs that write programs. With this strategy, you're seeking not just linear productivity gains but *compounded* gains, just like compounding interest.

To put this claim into perspective, consider the simple investing chart in Figure 2.4, on the next page. A double-digit investment edge (say, 10%) is a significant advantage. With a 10% investment edge over your competition, you'll double his effort every seven years. With a 20% productivity edge, you'll *double* his total effort every four years. I'm not suggesting you can compound all your development, but compounding even a fraction of it can lead to spectacular productivity improvements over time.

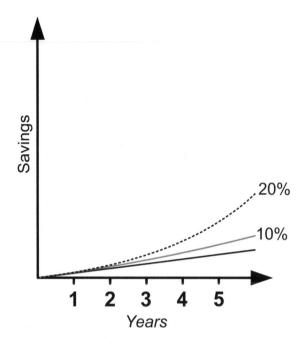

Figure 2.4: A 20% PRODUCTIVITY DIFFERENCE IS HUGE OVER TIME

Perhaps the best example of productivity is Ruby on Rails. By building features that eliminate traditional repetitive code and by concentrating on features that could reduce repetitive blocks of code to mere fragments, Rails has revolutionized database-backed web development. Each time I build on these features to add another framework fragment, I compound the productivity that's built into the Rails framework.

You may not be able to attack every project with an emerging framework like Rails, but you can still use Rails to give you a real competitive advantage by simply using it in spots. Each project you attack with a more productive framework, whether it's a smaller internal application or a custom one-time application for a customer, frees money that you could be spending on your main development effort.

Throughout the course of this book, I'll show you ways to use Ruby creatively side by side with Java projects. Each time you employ a more productive tool, you save money and squeeze your competition.

You've seen how you can take a more productive language and use it to your advantage. But the flip side is also true—your competition can do the same to you. With Java's dominance, dynamic frameworks such as Rails are not as likely to emerge in the basements of your competition. But as Java wanes, you have to watch your competition much more closely.

Taking Action

Deciding to choose Ruby over Java for a given project is risky. But remember, there are many levels of commitment. If you've recognized real pain, you don't have to negotiate a 50-foot drop to test the waters. At this point, it's probably more prudent to dip your toe in to test the temperature. Your goals are to begin to collect data, assess risks, and start to look at alternatives. These are tangible steps you can take, without committing yourself irrevocably:

- *Understand your problem domain.* If productivity is an overriding concern, choosing the right tool for a job is the most important decision you can make, by far. If you are starting a project that uses a web user interface to baby-sit a big, fat relational database or you're building simple tools to manage text, Java is not the right answer for you.

- *Count dollars.* Knowing exactly what a developer's day of work costs you is important and so is understanding the cost of a month of operations. With just this data and a pilot project, you can extrapolate a very good case for productivity. Counting all the hours spent troubleshooting classpath errors or the API of the month in Java can add up.

- *Get opinions you respect.* Talk to peers who have experience with Java and with alternatives. If you can't find one, find a reputable consultant who has that experience. Opinions are cheap when measured against the cost of poor productivity.

- *If you suspect a problem, collect data.* Many costs associated with Java are hidden. Complex issues such as bugs in frameworks or threading bugs are always difficult to identify and solve. You might be tempted to write those problems off as one-time occurrences. Don't. Record every second you spend solving them. Add up the time you spend to ramp up and train your team. Factor in the time you spend building infrastructure instead of solving your core business problems.

- *Have a backup plan to Java.* Since you're reading this book, I'm assuming your backup plan is at least partially Ruby. Whatever your plan, you need a serious alternative to Java to know what to do should Java rapidly start to fade.

- *Reassess risks.* Often, risks identified on the front end of a project are not accurate or complete. For example, in today's marketplace, if you're not incredibly productive, outsourcing is a risk. It may not have been a risk when the project started.

In this chapter, we've addressed pain: Java suffers from too much complexity and poor productivity for new and experienced developers alike. In the next chapter, we'll look at some of the benefits of the Ruby programming language. We'll get some rewards to weigh against the risks. You'll see more interviews from some of the industry's brightest programmers, and you'll have real benefits to weigh against the risks of moving to a new programming language.

2.5 Executive Summary

- You should establish a credible pain before you consider adopting Ruby.

- Java is not nearly as productive as we need it to be.

- Java's poor productivity comes from a C++ legacy and from an explosion of frameworks leading to confusion and bloat.

- Martin Fowler, a leading industry technologist, breaks down complexity into essential and nonessential categories.

- The nonessential complexity on the Java platform is unacceptably high.

*Simplicity is the final achievement. After one has played a
vast quantity of notes and more notes, it is simplicity that
emerges as the crowning reward of art.*

▶ Frédéric Chopin

Chapter 3

Establishing Your Reward

In such a fickle industry, programming languages remain remarkably
stable. Programming languages based on the C-language syntax have
dominated since the mid-1970s. In the previous chapter, you saw some
of the reasons that the Java language may be showing signs of age.
In this chapter, I'll make the case that programmers may be ready to
move, and I'll also show you who's making that move.

3.1 Momentum

For new programming languages, momentum matters, and Ruby is just
beginning to explode. You can't necessarily see growth in job postings
yet, but other signs point to real growth. To see the beginnings of this
explosion, you just have to know where to look.

Visionaries

If you know where to listen, you can hear all about the adoption of
leading-edge technologies well before the rest of the industry. If you
want to know where the industry is going, build a network of visionaries
you trust. Look at the impressive list of programming visionaries with
some vested interest in Ruby on Rails:

- *Martin Fowler, chief scientist at ThoughtWorks, prolific and award-
  winning author, and one of the most influential thinkers of our time.*
  He has been a vocal proponent of Ruby, and ThoughtWorks is
  using Ruby on projects. Ruby is a major growth initiative for them.

- *Dave Thomas and Andy Hunt, founders of the Pragmatic Programmers, authors, and publishers.* The Pragmatic Programmers are

investing heavily in several Ruby offerings including an impressive line of award-winning Ruby books.

- *James Duncan Davidson, best-selling author and creator of Ant and Tomcat, two of the most popular open source Java frameworks of our time.* James Duncan Davidson is using Rails within a start-up to develop a web-enabled rich application that will be the primary offering of that company.

- *Stuart Halloway and Justin Gehtland, authors, instructors, columnists, and founders of Relevance, LLC.* Relevance is offering a series of courses on Ruby on Rails and is offering Rails development services.

- *David Geary, one of the best-selling Java authors of all time and a key designer for several successful web development frameworks including JavaServer Faces (JSF).* David is speaking and blogging about Rails with regularity.

- *Richard Monson Haefel, once one of two voting individuals for the Java Community Process (JCP) and a best-selling author.* Richard recently led the Burton Group in a discussion with high-profile U.S. companies about Ruby on Rails as an important emerging technology. He has also published a paper about using Rails with Oracle.

Many others are moving toward Ruby. Today, visionaries are even more important than they have been, because visionaries not only can identify trends but also create them. The Internet gives this influential group an increasingly powerful voice to reach ever-broadening audiences. Blogs, online articles, and public forums all serve to evolve technology visionaries into technology influencers.

Like any other successful businessman, I have a circle of advisors. When a visionary adopts a technology, he is making a calculated choice on a technology, the potential for commercial success, and the support structure for the technology. Through listening to the right people, I've been able to predict some serious market movements, including the emergence of Java, the fall of EJB, the emergence of Spring (EJB's replacement for many customers), and the rise of Hibernate. In each case, I was able to invest my resources early enough in my business to achieve a major competitive advantage. You can do the same.

Framework	Downloads
Spring framework	280,787
Hibernate framework	520,061
Ruby on Rails	500,205

Figure 3.1: DOWNLOAD STATISTICS FROM SOFTWARE REPOSITORIES SOURCEFORGE AND RUBYFORGE FOR THE MOST POPULAR INTEGRATION AND PERSISTENCE FRAMEWORKS FOR JAVA, COMPARED TO RUBY ON RAILS OVER THE SAME TIME PERIOD

Downloads

When you're weighing the importance of open source software, the key metric to watch is the number of downloads. This metric does not translate directly to the number of customers because one customer can download a framework many times or one department can download a tool once and share it with the rest of the department. Still, there is no better metric. Figure 3.1 shows the download statistics for Ruby, compared to the downloads for the two most popular Java frameworks for persistence and integration. Ruby on Rails has been downloaded over 500,000 times, as of May 1, 2006. You can check the up-to-date statistics for the largest download source of Rails at http://gems.rubyforge.org/stats.html. Figure 3.1 shows an approximate number of the most influential Java frameworks against the most influential Ruby framework over the same period of time. The gap is closing rapidly and may well be closed by the time this book is published.

Books

Books are another important metric. Open source frameworks become much more prominent as you can find more books on the subject, and I'm more inclined to take them seriously as more people buy and write books on a topic. A typical successful Java book will sell 5000 units. Dave Thomas's *Agile Development with Ruby on Rails* was the top programming book on Amazon.com for a couple of weeks, and the second book was *Programming Ruby*. In recent years, Java books have had a hard time generating that much interest. Different publishers have five Ruby on Rails books in production today, and the Ruby programming language will have more than 20 books by the end of 2006. Tim

O'Reilly, of O'Reilly publications says Java book sales are stagnating and the growth in Ruby books is very steep. The Ruby language, driven by the Ruby on Rails catalyst, is experiencing explosive growth that's likely to continue. But there's more behind this movement than hype. Let's look at the engines of growth: productivity, cost, and rapid ramp-up time—all Achilles heels of Java-based frameworks.

3.2 Productivity

You might wonder why I've gotten so passionate about Ruby so quickly. I've noticed a remarkable change in my programming practice since I picked up Ruby. With Java, I had long since quit doing live programming in my seminars. I rarely coded Java production applications. I had a difficult time keeping up with the rapidly churning state of the art in Java, because the choices were overwhelming me. I coded infrequently enough that basic problems tripped me up, often for hours at a time.

Since I've tried Ruby, up to half of my presentations show live programming. The audience feedback has been tremendous. After only several weeks, I became far more productive in Ruby than in Java, and it amazes me that I've only scratched the surface. I'm coding production applications again, and I know that I can tap deeper parts of the Ruby language and get even better.

Sure, there have been problems. I miss JDBC, a common database API. Ruby's DBI pales in comparison, and there's no broadly accepted standard API across all databases. I don't have a world-class development environment. There aren't nearly as many jobs out there for Ruby. I spend more time finding Ruby programmers for the mundane tasks not cost-effective enough for me to do. But I like programming again, and I've been programming more than I have in the last five years.

A Case Study

Let me expand on the experience that Justin Gehtland and I had with a customer with Java and Ruby. If you've been in this field for long, you've often seen astronomical claims of insane productivity improvements. Object-oriented software vendors claimed tenfold productivity claims. Development tool vendors often claim to make you several times as productive. Even Enterprise JavaBeans claimed to make us more productive. So when Ruby on Rails advocates claimed they were from five to ten times as productive as Java developers for certain types of problems, I tuned them out. I had heard it too many times before to believe it. But eventually, I tried Ruby, and it has changed me.

Justin and I had been working on a Java application with three typical lightweight Java frameworks: Spring, Hibernate, and WebWork. We had taken four months to do what a .NET team took far longer to do. I worked on the data model, and Justin wrote the Java code. I called Justin to talk about possibly exploring Ruby on Rails for the application after some preliminary prototyping. Justin told me he had implemented the entire application on Ruby on Rails in four nights.

Now, the second time through an application will obviously go much more quickly, but differences this great are significant. Over time, our productivity held up. I estimate we were from five to ten times more productive. Something else caught Justin's eye. With minimal tuning, the Ruby version was faster. Although we recognize this performance test was not perfect, it's unusual that a Java expert who had written books about Spring and Hibernate could make a faster Ruby on Rails application, with no previous experience with the Rails framework or the Ruby language.

Justin then published his results in his blog. His experiences fueled a deafening roar of protest from the Java community. Justin has been a long-standing author and consultant, exploring some of the most productive Java frameworks with a near fanatical following, but it's amazing how quickly we can turn on our own when we hear a threatening message. The Ruby on Rails versus Java debate still intensifies.

For another example, consider the Java to Ruby rewrite, chronicled in the blog Following the Rewrite.[1] The blog features posts from project managers and developers from the development team of an enterprise application in the mental health-care arena. The undercurrent of the whole blog is the amazing productivity of Ruby on Rails. This blog, too, has been attacked with fervor.

The root of the debate is productivity. Java developers claim that tenfold productivity improvements just don't exist for general programming languages. Ruby programmers point out that if you move from a general toolset to a specific one (such as from a general text and networking framework to a web development framework), the numbers

---

[1]http://rewrite.rickbradley.com/ chronicles a rewrite of an Enterprise Java application to Ruby on Rails.

are much easier to understand. Ruby is an applications language. Java was based on C++, which was designed to build systems software. Ruby proponents can point to specific Java limitations and use specific Ruby features that make them more productive. Let's look at the deep roots behind Ruby's productivity.

Power

I'm a big fan of cycling. Since I've been following the sport, there has been one winner of the Tour de France—Lance Armstrong. He wins because, for whatever reason, he consistently gets a little bit more lever- age out of each tiny pedal stroke. Multiply that miniscule advantage by hundreds of thousands of times for a typical tour, and he wins tours. The pedal stroke for a programming language is the expression of one thought, usually in a line of code.

In several software studies, the lines-of-code metric is the one that will most often translate to tangible benefits. You'll find a number of stud- ies, both old and new, on this topic:

- In *Software Reliability* [MIO98], Musa et al. claim the total number of bugs in a program is proportional to the total lines of code. This metric has been studied to death, and most believe that the number of bugs is *at least* proportional to the total lines of code.
- In *Peopleware* [DL99], Tom Demarco and Timothy Lister claim the length of time it takes to develop an application is directly propor- tional to the lines of code.
- In an interview by John Udell, Bill Gates claimed "There's only really one metric to me for future software development, which is—do you write less code to get the same thing done?"
- Citing the previous Bill Gates interview, Tim O'Reilly, the creator of one of the most successful lines of computer books of our time, suggested placing more emphasis on scripting languages such as Ruby that do very well with the lines-of-code metric.

There are many other examples. Opinions are clear. Total lines of code matter, and Ruby code is many times more expressive than Java code. Each line of code represents an additional burden for your IDE that must parse them, for your build tools that must process them, for eyes that read them, for brains that must understand them, for developers who must keep them clean, and for systems that run them. Each Ruby line of code—each pedal stroke—does the work of four or more typical Java lines of code.

Consider a Ruby program that computes a Fibonacci sequence (or the sum of the previous two numbers in the sequence). This program:

```ruby
x, y = 0, 1
10.times do
  puts y
  x, y = y, x + y
end
```

gives you the following:

```
1
1
2
3
5
8
13
21
34
55
```

Here's the program in Java to give you the same result:

```java
class Fib {
  public static void main (String args[]) {
    int x = 0;
    int y = 1;
    int total = 1;
    for (int i=0; i<10; i++) {
      System.out.println(total);
      total = x+y;
      x = y;
      y = total;
    }
  }
}
```

This code is typical, but not nearly defensive enough. The Java program will actually compute the wrong value (silently, with no exception thrown) starting at the 48th number in the sequence, because of integer overflow. Ruby will continue to grow the number into a Bignum. Countless money-abuse bugs in Java-based programs originate from int overflows. Exception handling for each would maintain roughly the same proportions.

Overall, the total weight, or inertia, of a code base is directly proportional to the lines of code. You may be able to generate some of that base with a tool or wizard, but you still have to maintain the whole set; you may believe that other factors mitigate the total lines of code, but

Metric	Java	Ruby on Rails
Time	4 months, half-time	4 days, half-time
Lines of code	3293	1164
Lines of configuration	1161	113

Figure 3.2: PRODUCTIVITY OF JAVA VERSUS RUBY FOR ONE PRODUCTION APPLICATION

Java developers must still work much harder, using cumbersome techniques such as code generation or complex techniques such as aspect-oriented programming (which changes the syntax of the language) or byte code enhancement (which is complex), to achieve the same result that a Ruby developer can get with a simpler code base and fewer total lines of code.

In fact, Java developers increasingly have to take the time to implement language features that other languages support natively. These features have obscure names such as *continuations* and *annotations* (which were only recently added to Java). Although the names sound academic, they are becoming increasingly important to Java. For example, continuations are critical for building the next generation of web servers. Java frameworks such as RIFE and WebWork had to implement their own limited continuations for Java, while developers in more powerful languages like Ruby can use such support natively.

Figure 3.2 shows the productivity numbers that Justin published for our Ruby venture I mentioned earlier. Notice the four-to-one lines-of-code advantage of Ruby over Java. I'd expect these numbers to change based on the particular problem you're trying to solve.

You might expect such a terse language to be harder to read and maintain, but your intuition can be deceiving. Take a typical task of counting to ten. Compare Ruby's syntax:

```
10.times { ... }
```

to Java's corresponding syntax:

```
for (int i=0; i<10; i++) { ... }
```

In fact, many people find Ruby much more intuitive than Java, and easier to read, because it's closer to their native language. You don't have to work as hard to translate it in your head.

Java programmers lean on tools and frameworks to help them win back some of the productivity they are missing right now. Java supports excellent development tools. Ruby has gotten only its first few development environments, and for many reasons, Ruby tools will be harder to build. But Java's tools can't come close to closing the productivity gap. Ruby is just a more powerful language, so it takes much more Java work to accomplish most Ruby tasks.

Since Ruby is relatively new, it does not have as many frameworks as Java does. So right now, if you're doing a project that requires specific features that have good libraries in Java but not Ruby, you'll lose some of your productivity edge. That's the reason community is so important for the emergence of new languages. But remember, the proliferation of hundreds of frameworks is not always a good thing and not always conducive to high productivity.

Choosing between the dozens of Java frameworks to do web development, persistence, or remoting is one of the most frequent complaints of many of my Java students. In these cases, the weight of so many frameworks can decimate your productivity. Simplicity is at least as important as choice. And if Ruby frameworks give you everything you need, the power of the Ruby language will give you a significant edge.

You might be thinking that Ruby is just a fad, like parachute pants or pet rocks. Maybe it is, but new programming languages don't fire up and quickly fade away. They accumulate critical mass for niche status for a community, or they don't. Do your due diligence. If you find that a language meets your needs, use it. Value productivity more and inertia less.

Figure 3.3, on the next page, shows you a few features that Ruby has and Java doesn't. I'm not going to bore you with the details. Just understand that these features all boost productivity, and they all let Ruby developers express ideas with more efficiency. I'll also tell you why they are important.

Long-Term Productivity

The power, simplicity, and flexibility behind Ruby's excellent short-term productivity also serve to sustain that productivity. Better maintenance comes from reducing repetition and expressing ideas concisely in a way that's easy to read and understand.

Closures:
> Reduce repetition and work with groups of items such as lists, files, or databases.

Pure object orientation:
> Ruby has exactly one type system. Everything is an object. There's less to learn, less to code, and fewer opportunities for mistakes. Pure OO makes your code easier to read.

Continuations:
> Make better web servers (probably the next generation of web servers).

Optional parameters:
> Allow better defaults. Ruby has a convention allowing a single table of parameters (called a *hash map*), letting programmers specify many different options only if an option is needed.

Open classes:
> Make it easier to test code and extend code in important ways that are difficult in Java.

ObjectSpace:
> Gives developers the ability to enumerate all objects defined in an application, improving debugging and allowing much easier implementations of certain algorithms such as publish-subscriber systems.

Freezing:
> Permits locking an object, to catch code doing something it shouldn't. For example, if a variable value is changing, you can freeze it and then let the Ruby interpreter tell you when someone else uses it.

Message passing and missing method:
> Lets you quickly add dynamic methods to an object at run time. For example, Ruby on Rails can let you use person.find_by_name_and_address or any combination of the attributes of a Person. Rails adds these methods automatically, through missing_method.

Figure 3.3: FEATURES THAT BOOST THE PRODUCTIVITY OF RUBY OVER JAVA

For long-term productivity, you also want a language that allows rapid extension. Dynamic languages have an excellent reputation for reducing coupling and for allowing extensions in ways that Java can't. In *Beyond Java*, I make the case that many cumbersome and complex extensions in the language (using buzzwords such as *dependency injection*, *aspect-oriented programming*, and *XML-based configuration*) are needed precisely because Java is difficult to extend in certain ways.

Finally, for long-term productivity, you want a language that is accessible to novices but available to advanced developers as well. Ruby allows conventional procedural programming for simple scripts, supports full object-oriented programming for the typical programmer, and supports advanced techniques like functional programming, metaprogramming, and domain-specific languages that are attractive to advanced developers. Ruby is good for both student and teacher.

Ruby on Rails

Ruby on Rails users claim that for a certain type of application—a web-enabled database application where the development team controls the database schema—Rails gains a significant edge with the following:

- *Convention over configuration.* Instead of forcing tedious XML configuration, Ruby on Rails relies heavily on conventions for naming and structure, dramatically reducing configuration. Figure 3.2, on page 42, shows the difference in configuration in our application.
- *A radically different database strategy.* A Rails program discovers the structure of a database and adds features to the application based on the contents of the database.
- *Providing excellent defaults pervasively.* The Ruby language offers better capabilities for providing default values, so most of the time, Rails developers don't need to specify common parameters but are still free to change the defaults should the need arise.
- *A rapid feedback loop.* Rails developers can change a line of code and then reload the browser. Java developers must often do special build or deploy steps. It's easy to underestimate the impact of saving five minutes dozens of times every day.
- *Built-in testing.* Rails builds default test cases and fixtures into the application. It's easier to build well-tested Rails applications.
- *Ajax.* Rails reduces the cost of building web applications with a feature called Ajax. With Ajax, your web applications can be more interactive, giving your users a more fluid, memorable experience.

The productivity of Rails goes well beyond bullets in a list. To understand the magnitude of what's happening here, you simply must have a development team, who has built web applications with other technologies, try Rails.

To have the broadest possible reach, productivity must extend beyond the production phase into maintenance. If you're looking for a productive language for the long term, you simply have to look beyond languages that may give you a quick productivity fix at the expense of long-term maintenance. Though disciplined teams can make them work, other teams experience a quick productivity euphoria with languages like Perl, PHP, or Visual Basic, but it all comes crashing down over time as the application slowly becomes too difficult to maintain.

So far, in my dealings with Ruby on Rails, the productivity improvements have been extended into the maintenance of the projects as well. All the developers on my projects can quickly understand what we've done, and make the appropriate changes. Ruby's advantages of an expressive and concise syntax, the wonderful readability, and the pure object-orientation serve us just as well in the maintenance phase as they do elsewhere.

I'll go one step further. I believe that Ruby's metaprogramming features, especially as they exist in Rails, reduce the kinds of repetition that make maintenance on software systems so problematic.

Inertia

The obvious rebuttal to productivity is reuse. If you can take existing frameworks and corporate assets, a common perception is that you can always be more productive overall, even with a less-productive technology. Witness the millions of lines of COBOL and CORBA (a distributed objects technology).

But if you're at all typical, you've spent way more money chasing reuse than you've saved, and modern reuse models, which we'll discuss in Chapter 6, *Bridges*, on page 95, will often let you reuse code written in other languages. JRuby and the simplified Ruby on Rails web services are two technologies that allow excellent reuse across language boundaries. If you want to be productive, you must be willing to explore the most productive technologies and use them where they make sense.

You can also expect to experience some pain related to ramping up on a new language. Keep in mind how often you change languages or add new ones—it's probably not very often. Inertia is a powerful force, but you can't let inertia hold you in a bad situation when alternatives are available.

3.3 Cost

A clean, productive programming language usually translates to lower bottom-line costs more quickly than you might think. I interviewed three business owners, discussing software development costs. In each case, the top costs all related to the developers on staff. The overall cost of an employee ranged from 1.3 times a developer's salary to two times a developer's salary, depending on the employment model of the company. By extension, improving productivity was by far the most effective way to reduce costs. And each said that he would be willing to use Ruby if it became clear that it was much more productive than Java.

Communication and Management Costs

Reducing the typical project size through improving your process or development language has some other benefits as well. Look at the ways a programming language can impact your overall cost structure:

- More productivity leads to fewer developers per project.

- You spend less effort on communication for small projects.

- Having fewer developers per project also lowers management costs per project.

- When you finish applications sooner, you deliver their value to the business sooner.

So, the overall reduction of cost is much more than just straight productivity savings. At some point, you can even realize exponential gains. Most project managers know that productivity degenerates rapidly as teams get very large. Jeff Sutherland, consultant for agile methods, provides a simple metric for team size: the average cost per function point across 1,000 projects in Rubin's Worldwide Benchmark database was $2,970. For teams of seven, the average cost was $566 per function point.[2] Several essays in the *Mythical Man-Month* make a similar case, suggesting exponential decay based on communication as team sizes

---

[2] Scrum Log, by Jeff Sutherland, SCRUM: Keep Team Sizes Under 7. Thursday, February 6, 2003

increase. The decreasing productivity of larger teams makes sense, because larger teams need to spend progressively more effort on planning, management, and communication, both within the organization and between the organization and external groups.

Take management. If Ruby on Rails is five times more productive than Java for web-enabled database applications and a manager can handle ten employees, a typical manager can handle five times as many projects. With such savings, you could flatten your organization by removing one full level of management.

Or consider communication. Software development on larger teams demands more design documentation. A family of software development processes known as *agile development methods* promotes relying on test cases and cleaner code rather than other design documents. These methods work best for small teams because each team must design all programming interfaces that will be used by other teams up front. This task makes up-front design work critical, but this design work takes more time, even though such documentation often becomes increasingly obsolete as requirements inevitably change. Then, the team must rigidly follow these public interfaces so that other teams will be able to use them upon completion of their code. Consequentially, larger teams lose some of their ability to quickly adapt to new business requirements. Further, the development cycle is longer, so new business requirements become more likely. Implementing late requirements means breaking the work of other teams, lengthening the development cycle again.

Multiply your productivity by just 2, and a large team of 14 becomes a small team of 7. You can manage it from one department instead of two, and you'll be free to use an agile process. Multiply your productivity by four, and a department of developers can do the work of a small division. If, at the same time, you decide to use top-tier programming talent instead of the typical corporate journeyman programmer, you'll see small teams of three or four that could do the work of many traditional Java departments.

In fact, if you look around, you can see a few prominent start-up companies spring up that adopt this exact model. The 37signals company that built Ruby on Rails builds web applications. In many cases, these applications would take many times the number of similar Java developers. They're getting incredible mileage from Ruby and from the Ruby on Rails framework.

The applications often heavily use Ajax, a technology that makes much richer web applications possible. These applications are very difficult to build using Java because the Java Ajax libraries are much more complex.

To put things in perspective, I joined a start-up in the year 2000 that did a project that was much less ambitious than Basecamp. Our company had 20 highly skilled Java developers. We bet on Enterprise Java-Beans. We were able to build our application and make it work, and it took us nine months. 37signals could have built the application in a fraction of the time, with no more than two or three developers.

Here's the kicker. A start-up that bets on Rails has fewer developers and delivers faster. Since their cost structure is so much lower, their capital will go further, and they'll have more funding options. They don't have to have nearly as much formal management staff. Self-funding often becomes an option. Sometimes, less is more.

The Time Value of Software

Any investor knows the time value of money. Dave Thomas of the Pragmatic Programmers believes in the time value of software. A deployed application should be earning you money or saving you money. If an application is under production, it's not delivering business value. If you deliver early, your solution begins to pay dividends early and frees developers to work on the next value-producing project. Figure 3.4, on the following page, tells the story for an ideal world. While developers move from one project to the next, users get the accumulated value of software you've already built.

But that's an idealistic picture. As your existing systems grow in complexity, you can lose productivity. And if your programming language and your software designs are too static, you'll spend too much time reworking the old system just to get to the point where you can add new features again. Some systems require more maintenance or more management expense. This is why productive languages that build clean, simple applications are so important. Every decade or so, as existing programming languages get more complex for the everyday applications we build, it pays to simplify and return to the point where completed projects deliver incremental value for incremental effort.

You've seen that the Java language is dated, but the Java platform's problems are not limited to the language itself. The Java frameworks

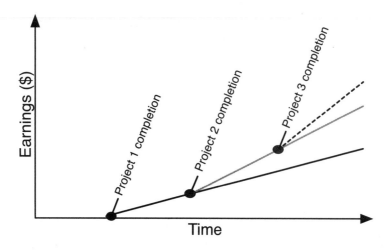

Figure 3.4: EACH NEW PIECE OF SOFTWARE DELIVERS INCREASING BUSI-
NESS VALUE

that allow Internet development and database access are cumbersome and complex by Ruby standards. Java's database access frameworks may be more sophisticated, but they leave behind temperamental, fragile applications. Java's enterprise-strength frameworks at best enable solutions to difficult problems at the expense of incredible complexity. At worst, Java's enterprise frameworks seduce users who should be working with simpler technologies.

3.4 Ramp-Up

The Ruby framework has still more advantages. You can ramp up developers much more quickly. Ruby, with enough framework code to solve the most interesting problems, is usually easier to install. A typical developer doesn't have to learn nearly as much. More important, most Ruby frameworks do a good job of giving novices some power right out of the gate and growing that power as they learn.

Becoming Productive

Though Ruby is an incredibly powerful language that's interesting to experienced developers, it attracts a wide array of beginners. The Ruby community has always embraced new developers, helping them out by answering questions and by creating the features you use to download and install frameworks. For example, the minute you decide to learn a Ruby feature, you can use Gems to download a project and all the features it needs. To install Rails, I simply typed the following and followed the prompts:

```
gem install rails
```

That's it. The Ruby installer called Gems went to the Ruby site called RubyForge and looked for the last stable release of Rails. It then automatically checked for all *dependencies*. (Dependencies include other projects that your project needs.) If Gems needs a dependency, it asks you whether you want to install that dependency. The result is a clean, simple installation process.

On the other hand, for Java, you'd have to download each project independently, making sure you had each dependency installed and configured. You'd often have to worry about environment variables such as the classpath, and installing the tools into your environment. Installing major Java frameworks is a major time drain. That's a shame, because installation is a chore that impacts every Java developer who uses a given framework.

After I downloaded Rails, I had my first web application written in 20 minutes. It often takes Java developers several hours to install and configure one framework, and a typical Java project may need five to ten open source frameworks. Getting a working application integrated across the frameworks is a major task. Figure 3.5, on the next page, shows the contrast.

Now, some experienced Java developers don't have to go through all these steps. They've taken the time to invest in a set of tools or skills that will manage that complexity for them. But learning an integrated development language, such as Eclipse, or a build management system, such as Maven, without knowing Java is an incredibly difficult proposition. Since neither the IDE nor Maven is part of the base Java distribution, the tools simply add to the piles of skills you have to learn to be effective in Java development today.

Too much reliance on tools also fragments the skill sets of Java developers and restricts the learning process. Instead of learning how Java works, the developer must often instead learn how Eclipse works with Java.

Task	Ruby	Java
Install a framework	gem install *framework*	• Identify all dependancies • install each dependancy • install frame-work
Configure	• Do minimal configuration • Run test app	• Make libraries available • Set variables such as classpath • Configure with XML • Compile and run test app
Choose a framework	• Few rich choices	• Many choices with vastly different trade-offs

Figure 3.5: RAMPING UP IN JAVA AND RUBY INVOLVES DRAMATICALLY DIFFERENT EXPERIENCES

Getting started as a Java developer today is traumatic. Many novice Java developers run into the same pitfalls. Configuring classpath gets us all at one time or another. Choosing frameworks from hundreds of possible alternatives is a daunting challenge in its own right, and ramping up on that framework can be oppressive too. Writing a "Hello, World" application, enabled for databases and the web, can take days or even weeks, depending on the choices you make. With Ruby, you could choose Rails, download it with all its dependencies, and have your first application running in less than 20 minutes. Free training videos can help you with the experience.

Education

When it's time to sharpen your team's skills, you'll probably find a similar experience to the ramp-up. Education is one place where Java used to have a decided advantage, because the Java language once provided an unmatched library for web development, and it was easy to find education from reputable sites. That advantage no longer holds. If you want to do web development with the state-of-the-art open source frameworks, you'll probably not be dealing with companies like IBM.

Instead, you'll be using smaller consultancies like JBoss Group, Interface21, and others depending on the tools you need to use. You may even need to use more than one consultancy to pull together all the expertise you need, which can get expensive. With Ruby, you'll be using similar companies to provide your training, but a single consultancy could easily have the experience you are looking for, since Ruby on Rails is an integrated development environment.

And when your team finally sits down in a classroom, they'll notice a remarkable difference between Java and Ruby. Visionary Stuart Halloway is excited about Ruby partially because it's such a good language for teaching.

Why is Ruby a great development language?
—A discussion with Stuart Halloway

Relevance, LLC

Q: How have you used Ruby to date?

I build database-backed, web-based applications with Ruby on Rails. This is primarily something that Relevance, LLC, does for customers and is certainly the sweet spot that has gotten Ruby so much press.

I also use Ruby for most of my Ajax development. I spend most of my time these days working in (and on) codecite (http://www.codecite.com), which is an Ajax-oriented outboard brain/presentation tool that I am building for myself (but will open source eventually).

Ruby's automation is underrated. Ruby + Rake is totally compelling compared to anything else of its kind. In the medium run, this may be more important than Rails. I still like building applications in Java; I *never* liked managing builds or continuous integration from Java.

Finally, to think in. Ruby has become my native language for solving problems. Those transitions happen only a few times per career (for me anyway), so it's always exciting when it happens.

Q: What problems are you comfortable solving with Ruby today?

Just about anything. We've had a few projects where the Ruby library we needed didn't exist yet, and we simply absorbed the cost of building the libraries as we went.

Q: What are Ruby's three biggest assets as a language?

First, expressiveness. Ruby code is expressive and readable. This is important enough up front, but even more important later: maintenance is a huge cost in the software life cycle, and Ruby code is easier to maintain. This will be a huge cost savings over time.

Second, the pragmatic and eclectic adoption of features from other languages. From a wide variety of other languages, you can come to Ruby and say "This has feature X which has always been really important to me, and adds idiom Y, which is very cool and new to me."

Third, Ruby is a natural fit for lightweight, internal DSLs. Ruby makes it possible to build a domain-specific language as you go. The sweet thing is that there is no clear-cut point where this happens; it occurs organically as you refactor code. The declarative syntax for relationships in Active Record is a great example.

Q: You've also been a Java instructor and author. What does Ruby do for you that Java can't?

Ruby is wonderful for teaching. Ninety percent of the concepts I want to explain to people can be explained in one slide, one paragraph, or one page of Ruby. That number is probably more like 30% for Java—the combination of XML configuration, static typing, long namespaces, and misguided exception handling makes Java a very difficult language to teach in.

As a higher-level language than Java and an interpreted one, Ruby is much friendlier to exploration. If you want to know how something works, you can simply type a few characters and see how the Ruby interpreter responds. With Java, you'd have to write, compile, and then debug your program. Ruby reads much more like English than Java. Take a look at these simple lines of code from Active Record, part of the popular Rails framework:

```
class Invoice ...
  has_many :line_items
  ...

class LineItem ...
  belongs_to :invoice
  has_one :product
  ...
```

You can immediately tell what's going on, without knowing too much about Active Record, Rails, or even Ruby. The Ruby programming language is packed with features that make it easier to read. Instructors who have taught Ruby and Java typically prefer Ruby, and it's easy to see why. Programming students can spend more time learning the programming craft and less time dealing with the mundane details of the language.[3]

In my practice, I can generally train a novice Java developer who has no Ruby experience to use Ruby on Rails (which has web and database components) roughly four times faster than I can train the same developer to build a web-enabled database application.

Higher Abstractions

A higher abstraction gets you closer to the solution of the problem you're working to solve. Ruby on Rails, for example, lets you generate a default application to manipulate a single relational database table from a web-based user interface; therefore, my students can get something off the ground quickly, within the first two hours of a Rails class. I can then help them experiment and extend this foundation. The experience for the student is at once motivating and liberating.

For example, Figure 3.6, on the following page, shows a simple example of a screen built to manage a database table of users. The application has four windows and took three minutes to build. The application is

---

[3]See *Learn to Program* [Pin06]

Figure 3.6: A SIMPLE RAILS USER INTERFACE

not nearly complete, but it gives me a much greater head start than traditional Java-based frameworks. By contrast, my advanced Spring Java course has my customers completing a database-backed web application at the middle of day three. The difference in the body language of my students is striking.

By letting programmers focus on customization and the intricate relationships between models, Rails greatly improves productivity for both advanced developers and students alike. Ruby is a more productive language, and Rails gives developers a better head start, without sacrificing good design techniques. Put them together, and you have a stunningly productive environment that accelerates productivity and doesn't let up.

3.5 Risk

You've seen that Ruby will usually have a huge productivity edge over Java when applied to the right problems, but you have to weigh those gains against increased risk. New languages are inherently risky. But if you do an honest assessment of risk, you'll find that though the Java language may be established, other factors increase your risk dramatically.

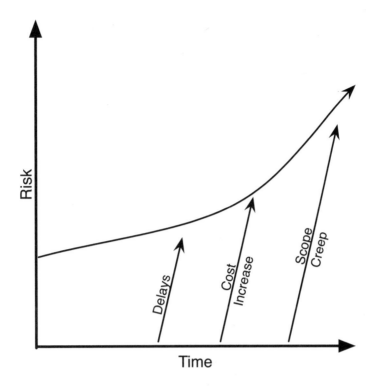

Figure 3.7: RISK INCREASES OVER TIME

Java's Low Productivity

All things being equal, the more productive language is much less risky. You don't have to look far for the reason. Risk increases with time (see Figure 3.7). Think of time as the perfect medium for disease. Time lets problems fester and grow. Longer cycles increase doubt and decrease morale. When you take too long, you overspend and open the window for scope creep, forcing even more cost overruns and new requirements. Time also opens windows for competition. All of these diseases take time to grow.

Java's Fragmentation

It's amazing to me that so many people fear the risk of a new programming language and yet have no problem at all with adopting incredibly complex frameworks that bind applications to an architecture until the end of time, or at least the end of the project. The Ruby language is relatively new (or, at least, new to most of us), increasing its risk. But compare that risk to the commitments you make within the Java community every day. Do you want to commit to Spring or EJB 3? Should you use Hibernate for persistence, JDO, or EJB? What should you use for the web tier? Struts, the JSF standard, or something more revolutionary? Some of these frameworks will fail, and wrong decisions can cripple you. Although the Java language may be safe, it's hard for even experts to choose the most effective frameworks.

At one point, experts have broadly promoted technologies that we now know to be mistakes, such as EJB. Big companies bet on this framework and sold it to their customers. I think similar mistakes may be brewing for very popular frameworks such as web services, JavaServer Faces, and JavaServer Pages. Each major architectural layer of a typical Java application offers a choice of dozens of possible technologies. Certain tiers of development may be fairly well established, but others, like the web presentation tier, offer a staggering lineup of choices—Struts, JavaServer Faces, WebWork, Tapestry, Rife, Spring Web MVC, and many others. On this tier, the safe choices are among the least productive.

By contrast, Ruby is relatively consolidated. Most Ruby development occurs on Ruby on Rails. This framework consolidates frameworks for persistence, user interfaces, web services, security, XML, and even e-mailing. The choices may not always be as robust as the Java alternatives, but they are integrated with the overall platform, leading to rapid ramp-up and incredible productivity. You'll also find Ruby much easier to extend than other languages. So from a language perspective, the Java language is safe. But for frameworks, you could well make the case that Ruby on Rails is a safer framework than even the most respected Java stacks.

3.6 Looking Ahead

The Ruby language is exploding rapidly because it's so productive. Many Java visionaries are leaving the Java community to gear up for Java development. Although the productivity may not fully translate to all problem spaces, it's very real for applications that web-enable relational databases. Although new languages may carry more risk than older ones with similar characteristics, some factors such as cost, productivity, ramp-up time, and competition increase Java's risks significantly.

In the end, productivity is the measuring stick for all technologies, and the productivity reported by Ruby on Rails developers is staggering. If I'm looking at programming languages, a language that makes me two times productive is compelling, but we're hearing reports that Ruby on Rails is five to ten times as productive as Java for certain problems. I was skeptical until I experienced it for myself.

We've just concluded the data collection portion of this book. In the next chapter, we'll begin to discuss limited deployments, beginning with pilots. We'll work to understand various models for mitigating risk, looking at several pilot scenarios that have been successful for Ruby pilot projects in the past.

3.7 Executive Summary

- Gauge Ruby's explosive growth with downloads, visionaries, and emerging books.

- The cornerstone of the Ruby experience is productivity, both short and long term.

- Java's risk factors are perceived to be low because of dominant market share.

- But project risk increases with time and complexity, and Java fares poorly with both.

- Java is an infrastructure language that's ill-suited for many applications.

If you want to make enemies, try to change something.
► Woodrow Wilson

Chapter 4

Pilot

4.1 Building Your Plan

The first time you use a new language in anger, to solve a real business problem, there's much at stake. If you're wildly successful, you can pave the way for change. If you fail miserably, you may never get another chance. If you're convinced that Ruby can help, you'll need to carefully plan this initiation.

Identifying a Business Problem

You'll choose your business problem based on the political environment and technical demands. You'll need to strike a balance across at least two axes: the political and the technical. If you get too conservative and pick a problem that's too easy or too small, you won't prove much, and no one will take notice. Conversely, if you get so aggressive that you hit technical obstacles beyond your abilities, you could fail, or experience an ugly success and get swept away by politics. The interview on page 66 tells the story. As a problem gets more difficult, risks get higher, but you learn more. As politics and visibility increase, your potential reward gets higher, but consequences also increase.

Choosing a Technical Problem

Combined with the people you put on the project, the technical characteristics of your problem, more than any other characteristics, will determine your success or failure. A good tool, used for the wrong job, is a bad tool. Chapters 5 and 6 will explore Ruby technologies in greater detail, but let's look beyond the simplistic view of picking the right job for the tool. Figure 4.1, on the next page shows that your political goals will help determine the technical problem you choose:

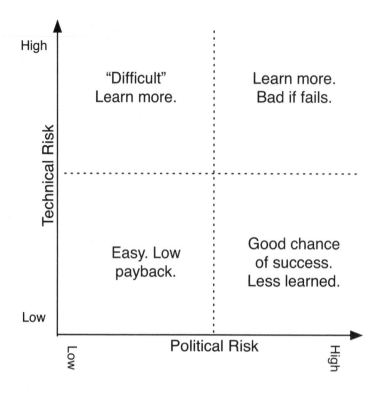

Figure 4.1: HIGH TECHNICAL RISKS ARE IDEAL FOR LEARNING BUT BAD FOR POLITICS

- *Selling.* If you've already chosen Ruby and you're looking to establish early success to sell the framework, you want the easiest possible problem and best possible fit.
- *Learning.* If you're more interested in learning about how far you can push Ruby or whether it's the best technical fit, then you'll want to pick a more demanding technical problem, and you'll want to see how far you can bend Ruby to suit your purposes.

In other words, you can't always have the perfect pilot for both selling and learning. Since you'll usually want to do some of both, you'll have to strike a compromise. As I lay out individual scenarios from teams who have built successful Ruby pilots, you'll see how each team considered both the technical and political realities of breaking new ground. You'll have to do the same:

- You'll be learning a new technology. You'll want to show off your productivity, but make sure you allow some time for your team to play and learn so you'll know more about the environment and have a better experience once it's time to apply your knowledge to a real-world problem.
- You'll often be tempted to explore some aspect of Ruby that other teams have never tried before, but you'll be much better off if you stick to problems that others have solved before you for your first project. The Ruby community is open and accommodating. Ask them whether anyone has tried a given problem before.
- You'll be anxious to prove that you can work on a thinner budget, but be careful. If you need help, get it. Working with a Ruby expert on a short-duration pilot project will save you thousands of dollars in the long run. You won't save any money if you attack too much of a problem before you're ready.
- Keep sight of your political goals. If Java is not working in your environment, your first goal is to establish a working alternative. If serious Java proponents exist, technical failure will be devastating, so you'll want to start slow. If you have more freedom to fail, you can push the technology into more demanding applications.

Building a Team

After you've chosen a problem, you'll need to build a team. The best teams for Ruby have a few common characteristics:

- *They often have some experience with dynamic languages.* If your programmers have written Smalltalk, Lisp, Python, or Perl before, they'll be able to take better advantage of Ruby. If they've used Java's dynamic features such as reflection or aspect-oriented programming, they'll fare better than those who haven't.
- *They are small.* You don't need nearly as many developers as you need for similar Java problems.
- *They have freedom.* If your technical staff is free to make their own decisions, they'll make progress more quickly.

Small, smart teams play to the strengths of dynamic languages. In the rest of the chapter, we'll lay out scenarios that have been successful for other Ruby teams. They will range from simple to complex on a technical scale and from low to high visibility on a political scale. See how others introduced Ruby.

4.2 Scenario 1: Classic Pilot

Using this scenario, your goal is to learn enough about Ruby to make a go or no-go decision. Frankly, this scenario is not quite as common as you'd expect. Since Java is near its peak popularity, language advocates typically need to be stronger and more creative than those for other new technologies. Still, a pilot project can often tell you everything you need to know about whether Ruby is a technical fit.

Profile

This scenario differs from the others in this chapter because the primary goal is to learn, rather than sell. Figure 4.2, on the facing page, shows that when you look at the profile for this type of application, the critical axis is the technical one. Although different people in your organization may well have different motivations, if your goal is to make a decision rather than validate your decision with a successful pilot, you're going to want to choose an application with enough technical challenges to make your decision. The political visibility of the project doesn't matter as much. For the best of cases, you should reduce your risk by picking a project with limited consequences for failure.

Example: A Manufacturing Monitor at Autobar Flexible Holland B.V.

Sake Lemstra, a managing director at Autobar Flexible Holland B.V., asked Henri ter Steeg of LinkIT Group to develop an application to help collect data on his manufacturing process. The interview on page 66 tells the story. Originally, Henri used Java with Swing to develop the application, based on the popularity of Java and the excellent enterprise integration features, including good Oracle integration. The performance was adequate and the interface was rich, but the application became increasingly complex as new requirements came.

They decided to pick a new technology and considered several Java solutions, but none of them seemed to offer enough of an advantage to make a rewrite worthwhile. Henri noticed the new Ajax support in Ruby on Rails, so he decided to give Rails a try. Henri was concerned about several aspects of the application that would stretch the Ruby platform:

- The performance would have to be good, because the application would post graphs with thousands of data points every minute.

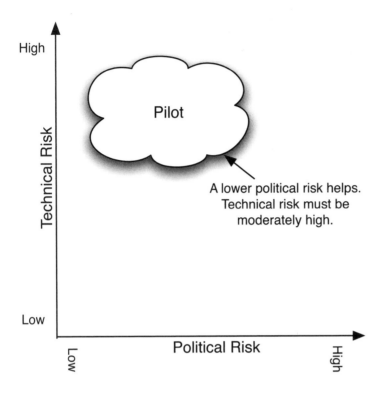

High

Technical Risk

Low

Pilot

A lower political risk helps.
Technical risk must be
moderately high.

Low

Political Risk

High

Figure 4.2: CLASSIC PILOTS NEED MEDIUM TO HIGH TECHNICAL RISK

- The customer had a version of Oracle that was not yet supported by Ruby on Rails, so they'd need to add specific support for Oracle features such as their outer join syntax.

- The user interface would need to be much more powerful than typical HTML applications.

Henri decided to implement a small slice of the application but one that dove deeply into technical details. He implemented a classic spike, which is a thin but technically demanding slice of the application to make sure Ruby on Rails would work. A custom caching layer solved the performance concerns. Ajax support, in conjunction with existing C code, handled the graphing functions needed by the sophisticated interface requirements. The flexibility of both Ruby and Rails allowed him to change the outer join syntax and add a simple real-time cache to his objects by changing the definition of classes in the core frameworks. This capability, called *open classes*, lends an incredible flexibility to Ruby, compared to Java. Because of excellent productivity and a much simpler application base, they decided to move ahead with Ruby on Rails. His customer was more interested in a clean, working application on a better timeline than forcing a Java agenda, so he moved development operations to Ruby.

Drawing Conclusions

Henri's implementation was a classic pilot. He was most interested in improving productivity and saw Ruby on Rails as one possible candidate to get him there. He was not concerned about political fallout, because had he failed, he would have simply chosen an alternative technology. This was strictly a learning exercise. The pilot was quite successful. Even after dealing with these framework limitations, Henri estimates that he is roughly four times as productive on Rails as he was in Java.

Rescue scenario—A discussion with Henri ter Steeg

LinkiT Group

Q: Would you describe your application?

We had a suffering Java application. The application was written in Swing. It worked OK, but it was getting too complicated. The application had to communicate with other clients, and we couldn't get it to query the database with good performance. It got to the point where we were afraid to add more features, because the application was out of control. So, we decided to move the application to another framework.

We looked at other Java frameworks first. We considered the *Spring Rich Client* framework, but it looked unfinished. We also considered a handful of other Java frameworks.

We ran across Rails. We considered it briefly and then put it aside until the Ajax stuff came along. I thought, "This is really impressive." I did a spike and was really surprised with the speed of development. I could develop client-server applications very fast. I got back to Java and said, "This is too difficult, and it's too much work."

On Rails, my development speed was excellent.

Q: What were some of the limitations?

We needed to use abstract data types for performance reasons. In JDBC, you can use them, but you can't in Rails. So, we created some views and "instead of" triggers and got past the problem. We also used Oracle drivers that did not support the outer join syntax. Active Record did not support outer join syntax, so we just created some classes and changed one of the Rails methods at run time. It was easier than I expected to work around what looked like serious problems at the time.

Q: What are you using for security?

At the moment, we're just using Apache security. We did not use the Rails generator. For now, Apache security is all we need.

Q: Have you been pleased with the performance?

For the most part, it has been good. We had one major performance issue. With Java, we could use a Swing app, which did some caching for us for performance reasons. This approach is difficult with a web app. We solved it with time-based caching.

Q: Did you experience any resistance to Rails?

No. The business environment trumped everything else. Our code is simpler and easier to maintain, and we can work faster with it.

Q: What were your top business priorities?

We wanted a stable application. We wanted to develop faster, and we wanted a simpler code base. As a very rough guess, I'd say we're coding three to four times faster.

Q: What was the most interesting part of your application?

We wrote a C fragment to produce our business graph. The business logic gets one data point for each minute, and we accumulate many data points over time. Doing a fresh database query every minute was not an option. In the Swing application, we cached the entire graph. Now, database triggers write the new data points to a file. We have a CGI script that reads the file and plots the graph.

4.3   Scenario 2: Trojan Horse

With the Trojan horse strategy, your goal is to get a working pilot established with minimal visibility and leverage that tiny success to increase Ruby penetration. Unlike the classic pilot scenario, you're not as interested in learning from the experience. You've already established that Ruby can help by other means, and you're seeking to establish some success with an easy project with a political climate that will not provide much resistance. If you later choose to do so, you can grow your advocates internally and leverage your success for better Ruby penetration on more important applications in the future.

Profile

The key to the Trojan horse scenario is to get your initial pilot, or Trojan horse, established with as few technical and political obstacles possible. To do so, you work Ruby into an organization with very little management visibility and feed the Ruby development culture. You'd prefer an application with little technical or political risk, as in Figure 4.3, on the facing page, choosing instead to fly Ruby in beneath the radar. Culture is often the most important element. You want to build a groundswell of support for the language from the bottom up.

Keep in mind that you'll need to take on enough technical risk to prove something important—you won't prove anything by building an application to manage your ten contacts with a primitive web page. Often, you're looking to save time and money by efficiently handling tedious, unimportant jobs, where technology choice might not be as much of an issue. These applications are often inward facing and may support other applications. Admin consoles, tests, and build tools are likely targets for the Trojan. You can then promote your success and leverage that success to take on other Ruby on Rails projects.

Example: Amazon.com

The Amazon.com interest in Ruby has been well publicized by several bloggers, including Steve Yegge, who worked at Amazon.com for seven years (and provided much of the background for this scenario), and David Heinemeier Hansson, the creator of Ruby on Rails. Ruby was initially not a popular or approved language at Amazon.com, but they have since hosted the Seattle-area Ruby user group. To establish Ruby, its proponents simply got Ruby into the hands of developers who could use it. The tools support team made sure Ruby was installed on all

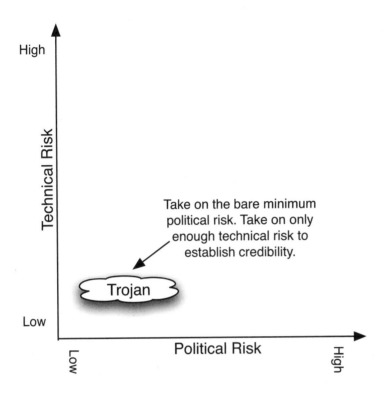

Figure 4.3: THE TROJAN HORSE SCENARIO REQUIRES LOW RISK ON BOTH AXES

developer machines. They brought in Dave Thomas to do a brown-bag talk on Ruby. Dave didn't actually promote using Ruby at Amazon.com; instead, he promoted learning alternative languages to learn how to program better. They gave away 120 free copies of *Programming Ruby* [TFH05] and eventually built a ground swell of support at Amazon.com. Ruby found increasing use in small, inwardly facing projects. Ruby is thriving today at Amazon.com as an accepted language, though it does not do most of the heavy lifting.

Example: An Administrative Console

I recently encountered another excellent opportunity for the Trojan horse strategy. I was doing a Java training course at a consultancy. They provided application developers to conservative companies. Nearly all their development was done in the Java programming language. One

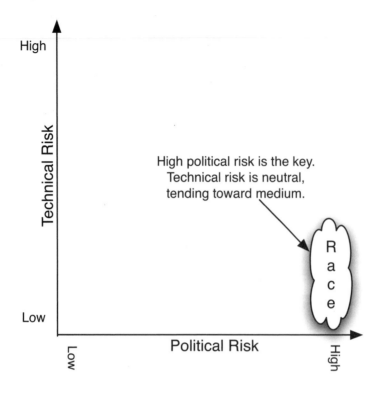

High political risk is the key.
Technical risk is neutral,
tending toward medium.

R
a
c
e

Technical Risk — High / Low

Political Risk — Low / High

Figure 4.4: THE RACE OFFSETS HIGH RISK WITH A JAVA HEDGE

application in particular was done with old technologies, including EJB. The project ran over budget, and they ran out of time and money before they could implement their administrative console. Instead, they asked their customers to manipulate data in the live production database with raw SQL statements. They were concerned that they were opening up their database to data entry errors and possible integrity problems.

Throughout the course, we discussed the application and came to the conclusion that though the customer was a Java-only development shop, the client would be receptive to installing a Ruby administrative console, because it would take a fraction of the cost to develop the administration console in Java. In fact, most of the application could be generated by Ruby on Rails directly, without much customization at all. I don't know whether the customer has yet moved forward with this approach, but it would be an outstanding example of the Trojan horse scenario.

4.4 Scenario 3: Race

A rapidly growing strategy for selling Ruby on Rails into conservative organizations is based strictly on the incredible productivity of the platform. With a race between Java and Ruby, you can turn a pilot that would be a high-stakes gamble into a relatively safe and very effective way to introduce Ruby. Your goal is to implement a Rails application and a Java application side by side. If you pick a problem that's as good a fit for Ruby as Java, the Ruby team will usually show far better productivity. The race scenario is attractive across a broadly different set of circumstances:

- *Improving technical fit.* For applications where Java is a particularly bad technology choice and Ruby is a good one, the Race scenario works well. Ideal Ruby on Rails applications, with well-defined and simple integration scenarios, are the most common.

- *Improving options for consultancies.* If you think Ruby is the best technology choice but the customer balks, you can often take a financial risk. Implement the Java project and Ruby projects side by side, and show the customer what you've achieved. They may be willing to buy the Ruby version from you or pay you higher hourly rates to make up the difference once you've proven the success of the platform.

- *Winning over upper-management.* If lower-level management supports Rails but higher management doesn't, you can spend your contingency budgets on Ruby as your hedge. Developing a backup application is a viable way to mitigate risk. It's much tougher for upper-management to reject a proven development effort.

Profile

Figure 4.4, on the preceding page, shows that a race scenario depends on middling technical risk and very high political risk. You're willing to take on higher risk by using a more important application because you have the Java project as a hedge. If you fail, you can simply continue development with the Java version.

The downside is cost, but since the Ruby project should take far fewer resources, it should be incremental to your overall Java costs. The core question is this: who pays? You've seen that consultancies may be willing to foot the short-term bill, betting that the customer will pay for the effort so far, once you're far enough along to prove your value.

If you're the project director, you may be willing to spend your research or contingency budgets on a parallel development effort.

Alternatively, you can sell the Ruby development as a cheap hedge. You have to be creative. It's usually difficult to get conservative management to sign off on risky technologies, and is doubly so for parallel throwaway development, but it can and has been done.

Example: A Start-Up Company Builds a Manufacturing Application

J2Life, LLC, and Relevance, LLC, worked together on an application for a start-up in the spring of 2005. We began building the application with the lightweight stack of Java frameworks including Spring, Hibernate, and WebWork. I worked on the data model and advised the customer. Justin worked with the remainder of the code. The customer, a start-up in Austin, had been complaining about the slow pace of new development and our responsiveness to changes. He was self-funding, and the application was the company's only asset. The intelligence of the application was in the organization of the data model based on the years of experience of the founder. We basically needed a web user interface to manage a relational database.

Justin and I both experimented with Ruby on Rails after talking to Dave Thomas at a conference. I played enough to find that we should take Rails seriously. Justin actually completed all the functionality that we had built in Java, but in a fraction of the time. The start-up company's goal was to sell the technology to large manufacturing companies. We were confident that large manufacturing companies would be willing to buy a Ruby application.

When we talked to the customer, we were able to show overwhelming productivity improvements and the corresponding lower cost. We shifted to a reduced, fixed-price contract, which also pleased the customer. By doing so, we eliminated the customer's downside risk, and Relevance improved their margins, because the newer technology was so productive. They passed additional savings on to the customer as well.

This project eventually failed, but not for technical reasons. Considering the eventual failure, we believe the Rails choice was well justified, because we limited the out-of-pocket expenses from the investors.

Over time, Justin's productivity was between five and ten times his productivity with the Java programming language. He found that the Ruby version of the application could be tuned for performance much more easily than the Java version, and with the Ajax support, the user interface was better also.

Example: Consultancies

I have recently learned that we are one of several consultancies that have used this Race scenario. In two cases, the consultancy initially funded the Ruby development effort. They were willing to do so to gain experience with the exploding Ruby language. Like Justin and I, they also had enough confidence in the Ruby on Rails technology that they fully expected the investment to pay off.

In every case, the customer had struggling Java development issues, usually due to the complexity of building web-based applications in Java. As I did the research for this book and *Beyond Java*, an often repeated message was that the Java platform simply makes web development harder than it needs to be.

The Race scenario need not depend on web-based development. Small teams with strong experience with dynamic languages can usually work much faster than Java teams given a common problem set.

4.5   Scenario 4: Bet-your-Business: Basecamp

The riskiest, and potentially most rewarding, scenario is to bet your business on the productivity improvements you can get with Ruby on Rails versus Java. This scenario is actually more popular than you might expect among start-up companies. These types of companies need serious technological edges against larger competitors, and a more dynamic and productive programming language is often a serious part of the equation.

The Ruby on Rails project was basically built based on this scenario at 37signals. There, a very small team of programmers builds and maintains web applications that are used worldwide. The company is now viewed as one of the most promising young companies in the world.

In these cases, the risk associated with Ruby is trivial against the potential rewards of the environment. Figure 4.5, on the following page shows the profile.

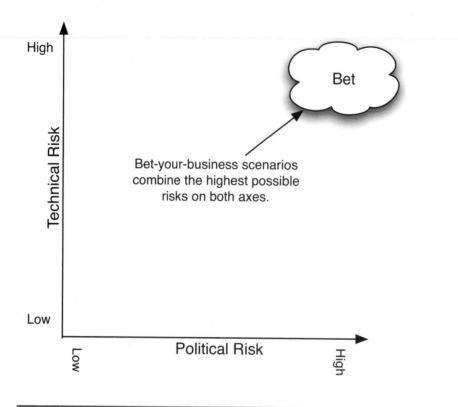

Figure 4.5: THE BET-YOUR-BUSINESS SCENARIO OFFSETS RISK OF A NEW LANGUAGE AGAINST GAINS IN PRODUCTIVITY

4.6 Scenario 5: Rescue

An increasingly prominent scenario with Ruby is the Rescue scenario. The goal is to take a floundering Java project and implement the project with Ruby. When I took a cardiopulmonary resuscitation (CPR) class, we were told that we'd have to press on the chest of a patient hard—often hard enough to break ribs. When we asked if that might hurt the patient, the instructor told us not to worry. The patient was already dead. The rescue strategy seeks to take a dead or dying Java project and successfully implement it on Ruby on Rails. Typically conservative management may be willing to accept an alternate technology to save the project. After all, the patient is already dead, or dying, so the risk is already unacceptable.

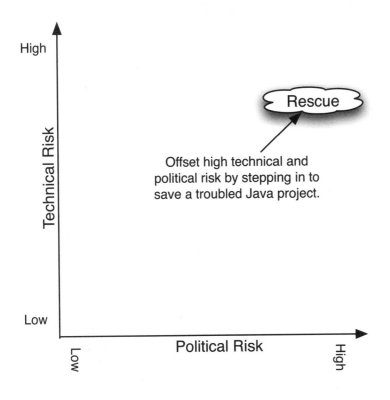

Offset high technical and
political risk by stepping in to
save a troubled Java project.

Figure 4.6: THE RESCUE SAVES A FLOUNDERING JAVA PROJECT

Profile

A rescue scenario takes on high political risk and a difficult technical problem, as in Figure 4.6. Your bet is that the high risk of the current project and the need for a recovery plan help offset the lesser risk of a new language.

You learned in the previous two chapters that risk levels increase dramatically with time and the risk profile of a newer technology reduces dramatically with market share. Here's the catch: you must make sure that the project is floundering primarily for technical reasons! If you don't have the skill or if the primary problems are related to the process, then a faster technology will just help you fail faster.

Example: Public Pilots at a Large .com

One of the largest .com organizations in the United States has a number of pilot projects every year to entice new customers to their existing services. Often, the designers of these aggressive pilot programs have no clear idea what their customers want to see or how their user interfaces should present new data. I interviewed a developer who works at this company. I knew he was a proponent of Ruby but didn't know he had been able to use Ruby at work. He offered this story, provided that I leave out details that might identify the company. We'll call my contact Bill and his company Mega.com.

Like many of the more successful .coms, Mega.com is a strong proponent of using good technologies. They've used Java extensively and also some other dynamic languages. Ruby has yet to be introduced. Bill had the charter of taking a small team and developing a pilot application with a proprietary Java and XML-based framework. After working through several iterations of the pilot, he calculated that they could not possibly make their projected deadlines, because the Java technology was not nearly productive enough to handle the quickly changing requirements driven by their beta customers.

He told his management team that Java was no longer an option and he intended to use Ruby on Rails for the pilot projects. His choice paid off almost immediately, experiencing a fivefold improvement over the proprietary Java framework. Bill was shocked, because his team did not have working experience with Ruby on Rails, but they were able to quickly ramp up and generate the pilot application, learning as they developed. Bill estimates that his team will experience an order of magnitude improvement in productivity once everyone on the team is comfortable with Ruby and the Rails environment. He attributes this improvement to the programming language, the excellent Ajax integration, and the Rails environment. He calls Rails "the most important open source project in the last ten years."

Learning from the experience

Bill has some selling yet to do. Although he was able to push Ruby on Rails through for his pilot project based on the rescue scenario, Mega.com has not yet agreed to push Ruby on Rails into production. Because the Mega.com company has a strong Unix tradition and experience with dynamic languages, he has a fighting chance, but Bill now needs to do some research to back up his case for putting Rails into production. As with all .coms, a new service might have limited scalability requirements, but one post on Slashdot can increase volumes quickly to massive proportions. He's still doing research to make his case. Since Bill ran his pilot, many other teams at Mega.com have moved forward with their own Rails experiments.

4.7 Making the Choice

In the end, your circumstances will determine your decisions. Keep in mind that new technologies can and do fail. The best you can possibly hope to do is understand how much political risk you're willing to accept and weigh your potential gains against that risk. Keep in mind that even in the context of each scenario, you'll need to work to mitigate risks by picking the right team and making sure they are prepared for the challenge. In the next chapter, we'll talk about the technologies that come into play as you move from Java to Ruby.

4.8 Executive Summary

- Any effective pilot must take into account current technical and political realities.

- The goals of learning and selling are often at odds.

- A classic pilot undertakes a project with high technical risk and emphasizes learning over selling.

- The Race scenario runs the same project side by side with Ruby and Java.

- The Trojan Horse scenario seeks to introduce Ruby under the radar via low-risk, low-visibility projects.

- The Bet-your-Business scenario is common in start ups, and offsets the high technical risk of a new language with very high productivity.

- The Rescue scenario implements a failing Java project in Ruby, weighing high political risk of a new language against the higher risk of a failing application.

Chapter 5

On an Island

After you've implemented a successful pilot, you'll want to expand Ruby to other projects. This chapter and the next deal with the Ruby landscape and enterprise integration strategies. In this chapter, we'll talk about ways to build "island" applications that need very limited integration with the outside world. In the following chapter, we'll talk about the technologies that can help you integrate with other applications, Java and otherwise.

5.1 Overview

Many people have tried to pigeonhole Ruby into the niche of scripting languages. The implication is that as a mere utility language, Ruby will never form the foundation of real applications. As you've seen, a growing number of developers are pushing Ruby into ever-expanding niches. Ruby on Rails is a big part of that movement. Rails is an incredible framework that has excellent support for simplified but powerful web development, productive database access that includes migration of both your schema and data, web services, and even Ajax. But Ruby goes far beyond Rails. Ruby is an outstanding language for the following:

- Driving testing
- Integrating enterprise applications
- Working with text files
- Using images
- Building and accessing web services
- Using middleware like LDAP directories
- Working with databases

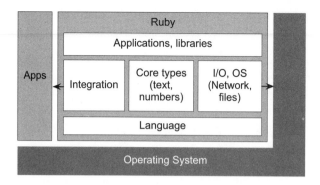

Figure 5.1: RUBY'S BASIC FEATURES

...and much more. Even without Rails, Ruby is a far more advanced language than Java for web development, as you will see. At some point, you're going to want to fly over the landscape at 10,000 feet and take it all in. This chapter will walk you through the most important and popular Ruby frameworks.

5.2 The Basics

Like Java, the Ruby programming language has been around for more than ten years, spending the first five years in relative obscurity, pretty much exclusively in Japan. Over that time, Ruby grew an impressive set of features. Figure 5.1 shows the major features of Ruby (but doesn't necessarily reflect the underlying structure of Ruby). You can divide Ruby's core libraries into these major categories:

- *Language support.* These features are the basic building blocks of Ruby, such as the syntax, expressions, threads, decisions, and loops. These features also support objects and the components that define objects such as methods and classes. In addition, language support includes the most basic and pervasive objects with containers to hold them. The language support tends to be more dynamic than you'll find for Java.

- *Input/output (I/O).* Ruby supports basic input and output features. I/O forms the cornerstone of any language. Ruby's I/O features allow access to devices and other programs. Borrowing features from both Perl and C, Ruby has an impressive and consistent library of input/output features.

- *Data munging.* When you add Ruby's impressive array of features dedicated to processing text and other kinds of data to the strong input/output features inherent in scripting languages, you have a language that's very well suited for data manipulation tasks of all kinds. Ruby's high-level string support includes regular expressions and advanced features such as templating (for tasks similar to mail merge) and first-class ranges that work with both characters and numbers. Ruby also has extensive support for math.

- *Communications.* Ruby supports common Internet communication via several libraries. For starters, you can use low-level Internet protocols such as TCP/IP and HTTP. You can also use higher-level APIs such as SOAP or web services. (We'll cover these features in more detail in Chapter 6, *Bridges*, on page 95.) Several web development features, such as the common gateway interface (CGI), are also supported. Combine this support with the templating support described in data munging, and you have a good language for creating simple web pages.

- *Development support.* Ruby has several libraries and utilities to support developers. Ruby has an interactive interpreter that lets developers explore and play. Ruby also has libraries and tools such as Rake to help you build projects, unit test your code, document your code, and run benchmarks to show you bottlenecks. Tools such as Gems and setup also help to package, deploy, and distribute new code.

- *User interfaces.* Ruby has support for building user interfaces. Though not as extensive as frameworks for the Java, Microsoft, or Apple platforms, they are quite productive. You also have the luxury of several cross-platform GUI toolkits.

- *Security.* Ruby has some features that allow you to encrypt files, identify user input that might have dangerous hacking code built in, or lock down separate parts of your application.

- *Integration.* Ruby has features allowing integration to Microsoft tools, DLLs, and other programming languages. The C integration in Ruby is especially strong. We'll look at the special integration packages available for Java in Chapter 6, *Bridges*, on page 95.

You can see that Ruby gives you a good deal of power right out of the box. Many programmers use these features as a scripting language, writing small applications to process text files or even deliver simple websites. Joshua Haberman of Amazon.com speaks of using Ruby as a scripting language. Ruby is quite powerful in that role, but as Joshua found, there's far more to Ruby than scripting.

Introducing Ruby—A discussion with Joshua Haberman

Amazon.com

Q: How long have you been using Ruby?

I first used Ruby in college, about five years ago. I liked it a lot, but I was afraid it would never gain enough mind share to be more than a niche language. Mind share is extremely important for a programming language. Only when a language achieves a critical mass do you start to see the kinds of libraries, frameworks, and tools that you need to be effective. If you write in a niche language, no one wants to read or maintain your code. Five years ago, it looked like Ruby was destined to be one of those great-but-unknown languages, so I switched to Python, which looked like it was going to be the dominant language in this space.

Then, a year ago, Dave Thomas of the Pragmatic Programmers came to Amazon.com to speak about Ruby. His talk reminded me of what a powerful, expressive language Ruby is and how it really does stand out even compared to similar languages like Python. Also, by this time Ruby on Rails was really hitting it big and creating the mind share that earlier I worried would never materialize. I left from Dave Thomas's talk and immediately rewrote in Ruby a Python script I had been working on. I haven't written any Python since.

Q: What types of jobs do you use Ruby to do?

I have found Ruby extremely useful for the jobs where people have traditionally turned to Perl. Utility scripts, batch jobs, unit tests, monitors, log parsing, ad hoc programs, and prototypes are all jobs where Ruby has been a powerful tool. In this space, Ruby is a clear win because it has all the capabilities of Perl but a much cleaner design and more expressive syntax.

I am also using Ruby on Rails to build an internal website. For a while I was skeptical about the buzz surrounding Rails, but now that I've used it, I have to say that it really lives up to the hype. Web applications have been unnecessarily painful to write for a long time. Ruby on Rails frees you from having to write the part of the web application that was always the most boring and unnecessarily time-consuming.

Q: Does Ruby make you more productive, and why?

If you see Ruby's most visible advocates speak (Dave Thomas and David Heinemeier Hansson especially), you'll notice that they talk about the happiness, joy, and motivation that Ruby brings to programmers. This may seem like fluff or icing on the cake, but for me it has led to very tangible productivity gains. I tend to be a perfectionist when I code, and I am always looking for the clearest way to express every line of code that I write. When a programming language doesn't give me a good way to say something, it's like writer's block—I have to stop my train of thought and dumb down my idea until the programming language can understand it.

On the other hand, if my language gives me a concise, readable, and elegant way to say something, I am pleased with what I've written, and I am inspired to continue writing.

Q: What's the best way for an established company to get started with Ruby?

I started using Ruby because it could make my job, as an engineer, easier. I focused my efforts on creating libraries that can interoperate with our internal systems, and I made these libraries as easy as possible to use. Once I had that going, I could start demonstrating to others that Ruby would make their jobs easier too. It is a very grassroots, bottom-up movement.

When I was first using Ruby, I would choose Ruby to solve small tasks that my manager assigned, being sure to let my manager know I was doing this. Over time, my manager noticed that when I chose Ruby, I would complete the job quickly and effectively. That made him more comfortable when I would choose Ruby for slightly bigger and more important programs. I definitely don't believe in springing a new language on an organization by immediately choosing it for something big. It needs to prove itself with small problems first, and management needs to be in on the conversation.

5.3 Web Development

People new to Ruby marvel about how an incredible web development environment could come out of nowhere to challenge the most successful programming language of our time. But Ruby was often used as a language for building simple web applications for most of its early existence. Before we look at Rails in detail, we should look at the Ruby technologies that are attractive to web developers. We should start with a discussion of a growing alternative to Java in LAMP.

LAMP

Many experts associate the Ruby language with a development strategy called LAMP, which stands for the open source projects Linux, Apache, MySQL, and Perl/PHP/Python. (Ignore the kickstand, and Ruby is a P-language too.) LAMP web development tends to have a few overriding characteristics:

- Open source software
- Web-enabled database applications
- Simplicity
- Low cost
- Dynamic programming languages

Figure 5.2, on the next page, shows a typical LAMP configuration. LAMP architectures work by running simple scripts through a web server. The web server uses the operating system to execute these scripts, usually through some variation of an interface called CGI. The scripts are simple applications that may access a database or file, execute some code, and add the results to a web page, which is then returned to the user. Since web pages are basically strings and references to static resources like graphics and music files, languages that are good at manipulating text tend to be good for LAMP.

Enterprise applications can have trouble scaling because as the number of requests grow companies must deploy the applications to more and more servers. Running the same application across several servers gets especially difficult when the application must share the resources across servers. Then, the complexity gets out of control, or the scalability suffers. LAMP achieves scalability through clustering, but applications don't share resources across a cluster. Instead, each application contains enough information to fulfill a request independently. Called *shared-nothing*, this strategy greatly simplifies applications and makes

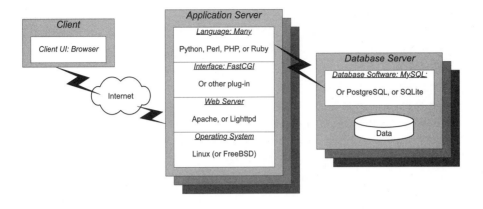

Figure 5.2: TYPICAL LAMP DEPLOYMENTS USE SIMPLE, SHARED-NOTHING ARCHITECTURES

it possible to scale by adding hardware. The networking infrastructure shares jobs across a cluster. Only a few specialized layers, such as the database or a distributed file system, are shared across the cluster. Everything else is private.

Ruby web applications typically use the LAMP approach. Ruby has many characteristics that make it outstanding for LAMP designs:

- Ruby is an open source language.
- Ruby handles text extremely well.
- Ruby supports all the necessary Internet protocols.
- The two most popular LAMP servers run Ruby, and Ruby also has a lightweight server for development.
- Ruby has efficient database integration.

Before Ruby on Rails became popular, many Ruby web applications used the LAMP style of development. Recently, some consultants and writers have suggested that LAMP technologies are starting to pose a credible alternative to the Java programming language and frameworks. Some of the most scalable Internet sites in the world, such as Google, use LAMP philosophies in places. LAMP technologies also have strong publishers available to help manage the community that makes programming languages and frameworks thrive. But web development still has some significant problems, and Ruby's developers are always trying approaches to take LAMP to the next level.

Continuation Servers

Web development has needed an overhaul for quite some time. Stateless applications often scale better for the same reason that shared-nothing architectures scale better. So, most web servers use stateless architectures. The problem is that stateless web development is hard, because it doesn't automatically keep track of whole conversations. If an application has conversations that take more than a page, the application developer is left to manage state without help. So each time an application has a conversation with a user that spans more than one page, like shopping from a catalog, placing an item in a cart, and checking out, the application has to keep track of everything that has happened in the past. That's a tedious process, and a user can click the back button at any time, making the problem even harder to solve.

Ruby has several frameworks that experiment with a new and radical way of building web applications. Continuation servers use a language feature called *continuations* to make web development easier. A continuation captures the state of an application. Ruby supports continuations. Using a continuation server, the web server can capture and store a continuation for each application, with only a limited impact on the overall scalability of the system. Ruby has at least three such frameworks:

- Wee is a framework that uses a continuation-like approach but doesn't actually use Ruby continuations.

- Borges is a port of a famous continuation server implemented in Smalltalk called Seaside.

- Iowa is a framework started by Avi Bryant, the author of Seaside. Now, Iowa is maintained by other developers, but it still uses some of the concepts of continuation servers.

None of these frameworks is broadly deployed, and some are immature. Even so, it's worth knowing about them in case you run into a problem where state management is a serious problem. You'll want to pay attention to these projects as they evolve, because some experts believe that all major web development frameworks will eventually use continuations.

5.4 Rails

Although Java has many different web development frameworks that are broadly used, Ruby has one in Ruby on Rails. That level of focus and integration gives Rails an incredible productivity advantage. A complete treatment of Ruby on Rails is far beyond the scope of this book, but you'll need to know about the scope of exactly what this beast can do for you. Rails is an application development framework that focuses on building web applications to front relational databases. It is fundamentally a mix of some glue code on top of several distinct frameworks:

- *Active Record.* Rails performs all database access through Active Record, but you can plug in other persistence frameworks if you want. Active Record improves programming by discovering the fields and structure, based on some naming conventions, and adding certain things to your classes automatically.

- *Action Pack.* Rails uses a well-known strategy for separating presentation logic from business logic called Model-View-Controller. Action Pack handles the presentation aspects of Rails.

- *Action Mailer.* Rails uses Action Mailer to handle e-mail integration for features such as password support.

- *Prototype.* Rails can make extensive use of Ajax technology to do things like drag and drop and rich user interfaces on the Web. See *Pragmatic Ajax* [GGA06] for more details.

- *Action Web Service.* You can integrate Rails applications with applications written on other frameworks and languages with Action Web Service.

- *Ruby.* Rails makes good use of Ruby's capabilities. Rails uses Ruby's metaprogramming to make it easier to define database classes and for simpler configuration within Active Record. Rails also improves on Ruby's core frameworks for web development and for helping Ruby and HTML work together.

Figure 5.3, on the following page, shows how it all hangs together. When you take these well-designed components and glue them together in a convenient way, you have the recipe for success. We'll focus on Action Pack and Active Record as the cores of the Rails framework.

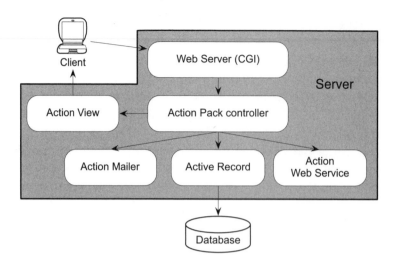

Figure 5.3: RAILS IS ACTUALLY A NUMBER OF SMALLER, LOOSELY-COUPLED FRAMEWORKS

Active Record

Active Record is arguably the most important part of the Ruby on Rails framework. It makes developing database-backed applications much easier. Traditionally, when you developed object-oriented applications that dealt with relational databases, you'd need to define the database and the object model independently and then write some code or configuration to tie the two together. Instead, with Rails, you simply define database tables and let Active Record automatically discover your fields and add them to your objects. So, an Active Record class looks like this:

```
class Book < ActiveRecord::Base
  has_one :author
  has_many :chapters
end
```

A similar Java class would be dozens of lines long and often require a configuration file as well. Active Record works by asking you to adhere to certain naming conventions in your database tables and in your code. If you do so, Active Record knows where to look for important information. For example, tables are English plurals of your classes. So, in the previous program, Active Record knows the class Book will get information from a database table called books.

You'll be much more successful with Active Record if you create your schema explicitly for Active Record. You'll have more limited success if you need to support an existing schema, especially schemas that have features such as composite keys, a strategy for identifying a row with more than one database column.

Action Pack

Action Pack is the Rails framework responsible for presentation. Action Pack handles both the view and controller parts of the well-known Model-View-Controller pattern. Views present data, Active Record models contain and store data, and controllers invoke both, moving data back and forth between models and views. Action Pack also makes sure that any incoming requests get from the web server to the right controller.

The Rails view framework is called Action View. It fills the same role as JavaServer Pages do for Java. Rails executes Action Views on the server, executing any Ruby code that plugs in dynamic content like database data from Active Record objects. Unlike Java, Rails developers are encouraged to add Ruby code directly to web pages, if it makes sense. Rails developers can then move code that has more to do with business logic into Active Record objects, whenever it makes sense.

Strengths of Rails

The developers I interviewed for this book love Rails. Most often, they cite incredible productivity gains over Java and other programming languages. You can attribute this added productivity to any number of small innovations, but a better explanation is that the integrated framework achieves a synergy greater than any single piece of Rails. The rapid turnaround between coding something and seeing it on the screen is also significant. The lack of repetition means less code to write, debug, and maintain.[1] Taken alone, each of these ideas is important. Taken together, they're nearly overwhelming:

- *Convention over configuration.* Rails achieves this improvement by taking advantage of the clean integration between Rails components. The difference in the amount of configuration that you need to apply to get a real application running is striking. I've measured

---

[1]See the DRY prinicple in [HT00]

a difference of ten to one on the production Rails applications I've worked on so far.

- *Scaffolding.* Clever code generation based on your model lets you quickly generate database-backed user interface code for a given database table to jump-start your development and get code in front of your users in a hurry.

- *Built-in testing.* Many developers recognize the need for writing automated tests, but it's often hard to jump-start a testing framework. Rails provides the project organization and creates simple test cases automatically, so you can build from working test cases to jump-start testing.

- *Tailored environments.* Rails creates environments for test, development, and production. Many frameworks try to optimize the development experience for either test, development, or production. But all of these environments have different needs, and Rails manages those different needs well. For example, the development mode lets you change a line of code and immediately see the result in your application, but the production mode optimizes for performance instead.

- *Domain-specific languages.* Rails includes a number of domain-specific languages that allow you to map application objects to database tables, create view components, and configure the application. Code written with these built-in languages is easier to write, extend, and understand.

- *Good integration with Ruby.* Rails uses the Ruby language very well. Sometimes, it's hard to see where Rails begins and Ruby ends. Rails also makes good use of Ruby packaging, documentation, and deployment components. This seamless integration makes Rails easier to use, learn, and extend.

You've seen that Rails is clearly the engine behind the explosive growth of Ruby, and the benefits do not stop at the technology, The Rails community is active, committed, and quite helpful. But Rails is not an island. Ruby has nice middleware integration capabilities, and Rails can take advantage of them well.

5.5 Middleware

Many of the people who explore Ruby for the first time are surprised by the number of available middleware integration packages. The roots of Ruby as an open source language of choice mean the most common integration problems have been solved. Many of the middleware integration frameworks use Ruby's interface for the C programming language, but some of the others have native support. This section presents some of the most important middleware packages.

Databases

Nearly all Java database applications access databases through JDBC at some level. Ruby has no overriding common database API, but there are still good integration strategies. Database integration with Ruby uses one of three strategies. You can work with a direct database API, you can work with a common database layer (like Java's JDBC), or you can work with a mapper. Let's look at each of these choices in detail.

Direct APIs

One of the features I miss most about Java as a persistence expert is JDBC, one common database interface. In Ruby, things are different. Many database bindings grew before any major effort was made to consolidate them. MySQL and Oracle seem to be the most widely used databases for Ruby, but you can also find drivers for many others. DB2, PostgreSQL, and Microsoft SQL Server all have database interfaces for Ruby, and many others are under development. Installing drivers for lesser-known platforms is often not for the faint of heart, but you should be able to find a driver for most commercial databases.

DBI

DBI, or Database Interface, is an attempt to build a unified database layer for all Ruby databases, using a library patterned after the Perl-based API of the same name. Python, Perl, and Ruby all use the same approach. A database specific layer, supplied by the vendor, accesses a database through a native interface. Then, a common layer sits on top, and application developers all code to the common layer. DBI represents an important attempt to unify database access on Ruby, but it has not been universally successful. Frameworks and application developers who need the best possible performance and stability tend to build on the native C database-specific drivers. Rails, for example, uses native drivers. All in all, DBI is moving in the right direction but doesn't seem to have the pervasive adoption of JDBC.

Mappers and Wrappers

Java developers tend to address higher-level database access with one of two methods. The first is object-relational mapping, and the second is database wrapping. With mapping approaches, you design your objects and database tables independently and then build a map between the two. With wrapping you start with a database table and then build an object explicitly to access it.

The mapping approach is by far the most popular approach in Java today. Frameworks such as EJB and Hibernate are by far the most popular frameworks for database access today. In Ruby, these mapping approaches are not nearly so popular. The most popular mapping framework is called OG, though the nature of the Ruby language makes it easy to write your own, so many customers have doubtlessly done so.

Using the wrapping approach, you create a database table and then create objects with operations that operate on the table. This is the approach used by simple Java frameworks called DAO frameworks. A couple of examples are iBATIS, Spring JDBC, and Velocity. Active Record uses the wrapping approach. As you've seen, the Active Record framework uses the capabilities of Ruby to build onto a developer's classes based on the fields and structure of the database. Active Record also handles relationships, while most Java wrapping frameworks do not, or do so poorly. You don't need to use Rails to use Active Record.

Security

Most Ruby developers use one of two approaches: they use Ruby's LDAP support to integrate to an external directory, or they use a plug-in for their web framework of choice. Ruby/LDAP is a Ruby extension that provides an API to access most LDAP servers. If you're using Rails, you'll probably use a more focused API instead. Several strategies exist to support security strategies that cover everything from flat-file support to database support to LDAP. You can also use Rails plug-ins to do role-based security or simple authentication. The choices are actually well developed and easy to integrate. Alternatives are getting stronger by the day.

Communications

Ruby has several available communications APIs. The most relevant are the low-level Internet standards and the web services. Since Ruby is not a dominant language, it must have a language-agnostic way to communicate with other applications written in other languages. Web services fill that niche nicely, and we'll talk about them in detail in the next chapter. Ruby frameworks tend to provide better support for a simpler model of web services called ReST, but support for SOAP is also available.

If you need to work at a lower level, you can easily do so. Ruby has direct support for the Internet's communication protocol, TCP/IP, as well as HTTP. You can also use a feature called XML RPC (RPC stands for *remote procedure call*). Some of the Java bridging technologies we discuss in the next chapter are based on XML RPC. Many other communication APIs at different levels are available to meet your needs, from CORBA to proprietary RPC. More are being developed monthly.

XML

Ruby has fantastic support for basic XML and a few XML-based frameworks like SOAP. Since XML is fundamentally a character string, the Ruby language is actually better equipped to deal with XML than is Java. Features like regular expressions, ranges, and Ruby's massive string libraries give it an inherent advantage over Java. You have several XML frameworks to choose from, but right now, the most popular is called REXML. It's loosely based on the Java ElectricXML package, but it's easier to use. If you depend on XML, rest assured. You'll have excellent support. We'll talk more about the XML support in Chapter 6, *Bridges*, on page 95.

5.6 Looking Ahead

So far, you've seen the tools you're likely to use to build stand-alone Ruby applications. Whether you use Rails or another Ruby web framework, or the simple CGI-based tools directly, you'll find a mature, effective language working for you. But all programming languages age, and eventually accumulate legacy code. And you may have your own legacy code to manage. In the next chapter, we'll talk about some of the tools you can use to deal with your legacy Java code. We'll build some bridges to these isolated islands.

5.7 Executive Summary

- The Ruby language has been wrongly pigeonholed as a scripting language.

- Ruby handles integration, data munging, web development, and other rapid development tasks well.

- Ruby on Rails is quick like PHP or Visual Basic and clean like Java.

- Ruby middleware supports database integration, security, messaging, communications, XML, web services, and more.

Design is not making beauty, beauty emerges from selection, affinities, integration, love.

▶ Louis Kahn, **master builder**

Chapter 6

Bridges

In the previous chapter, you saw how to use Ruby on an island. If you think of Java development as the mainland, sooner or later you'll need to build bridges to integrate your Java and Ruby applications. In this chapter, we'll introduce strategies for building and crossing bridges. Then, we'll show you the popular bridges from Java to Ruby.

6.1 Road Maps

When we were young, my wife and I used to be indecisive about eating out. We'd get into the car to just drive into town and decide where to go along the way. Often, we'd come to a decision and find ourselves on the wrong side of a river. We'd either have to backtrack or pick another destination, driving a long way to find the closest bridge. When we eat out now, we still get in the car and decide along the way. But we've learned where the bridges are, and we quickly vote yes or no to places that will take us across the river without a convenient crossing point.

Application development is like that. I've worked with many struggling projects over the years. Modern programming methods try to get you coding quickly with minimal planning, and that strategy works for small proofs of concept, and prototypes. But if you don't make important decisions early and plan carefully at critical points in time, your inertia becomes too difficult to overcome and can trap you on the wrong side of the river.

You've already seen what it takes to build a successful proof of concept. If you plan to leverage that early success to adopt Ruby more broadly, you'll need to stop and consider your overall goals. Your strategy will be different if you plan a wholesale migration to Ruby than if you plan to keep code written in multiple languages. And your strategy will change if you plan to mix languages within the same application rather than implementing each application in a different language, based on the characteristics of the problem. Let's look at various road maps that will take us across the river. We'll look at each strategy across two different axes.

Tactical versus Strategic

Tactical solutions are quick and usually simple but temporary or limited. Strategic solutions may be more complex or expensive, but they are lasting. Let's expand our bridge metaphor. When an army needs to cross a river without a bridge quickly, army engineers build a tactical bridge, possibly out of floating barges, knowing the bridge will probably not last through flood season. But when the City of Austin needs a bridge to serve generations, they decide to build strategically, carefully planning city growth, traffic flows, capacity, and impact on the environment.

Coming back to software development, a technique known as *service-oriented architectures* (SOA) is strategic, because it forces you to build the appropriate interfaces and extend your applications to use those services. A Java bridge is more tactical, because you can wrap a single method and make only minimal changes to get running fairly quickly without considering the sweeping implications of wrapping a method. You will often need to compromise between tactical and strategic, trading time against flexibility and staying power.

Coarse versus Fine Transport

Coarse-grained strategies seek to move big loads. They are often more efficient for moving great volumes through a system but are not as convenient. Fine-grained strategies seek to move many small loads, trading efficiency for convenience. For a metaphor, consider a company that must move great volumes of goods to the mainland from an island close to the mainland. They choose a location close to the best railway, because it's cost-effective, efficient, and frequent enough. Conversely, a person who lives on the island but works odd hours on the mainland will want to live near the road with the most effective highway bridge. Convenience is possibly the overriding concern. Sometimes you can get efficiency and convenience, such as rail transportation in some countries in Europe.

Applications are similar. If you plan in advance, coarse-grained integration can be very efficient. The Web generally works with coarse-grained communication. If you're building a user interface in Ruby that merely submits simple forms and accessing a Java back end with a web service, your needs are not too demanding. You'll choose a coarse-grained strategy such as SOA. You'll invest in a few common interfaces and design your applications to use those interfaces and take as few trips to the mainland as possible. But for some problems, you'll need fine-grained integration, such as scripting business rules in Ruby and placing them in a Java engine. You won't be able to afford the overhead of a trip across the network using an SOA, so you'll use a fine-grained strategy, letting both languages run in the same virtual machine.

6.2 Scenarios

Now that we've categorized strategies, let's look at some major scenarios. Your Java to Ruby integration technology will depend on your business problem. We'll categorize each one across both axes.

Migration

For a migration, you've fundamentally decided that Java is not getting it done anymore, Ruby is the future, and you'd like to eventually move all your Java applications to Ruby or shrink-wrapped software with some Ruby glue code to hold it all together. If you have a significant base of legacy code, you're going to have to plan on a healthy dose of migration. Your Ruby implementation strategy will depend on a variety of problems:

- *Integration between independent Java applications.* What kind of integration exists between independent applications? Are the integrations coarse- or fine-grained? If they are fine, can you switch them to coarse, in a pinch?

- *Time frame.* How long do you have to finish the migration?

- *Size.* If you have some larger applications, is there a way to break them up? Can you avoid a single big bang?

- *The urgency of changes.* Can you suspend changes while you perform the migration?

- *New functionality.* All projects need political wins. What easy features can you add based on capabilities in Ruby?

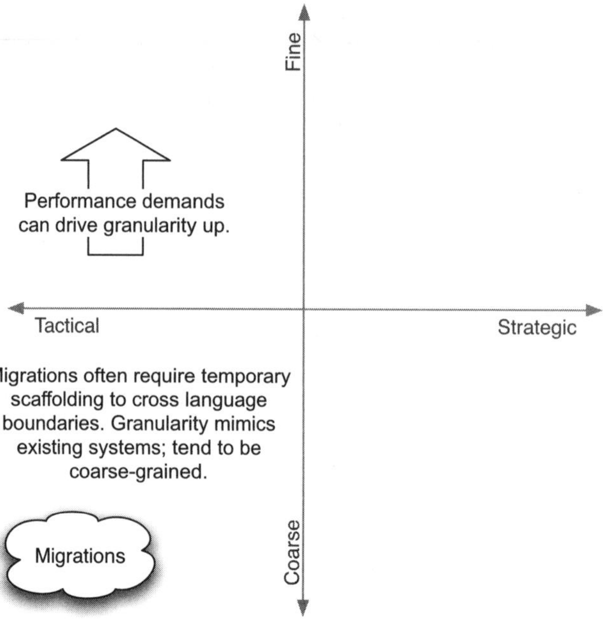

Figure 6.1: MIGRATIONS OFFER THE CHOICE OF TACTICAL INTEGRATION

Fundamentally, migrations have one thing in common. You will have the option of building temporary Java to Ruby technologies, as in Figure 6.1. Just like major construction projects, you may need some temporary scaffolding while your migration is underway. You don't have to take the tactical option just because you can. You might decide that an SOA could serve you well, regardless of language.

Keep in mind these issues:

- Big-bang migrations seldom work. Find a way to carve the project up, and iterate over each small problem.
- Migrations work best when you can deliver some unexpected benefit. With Rails, a richer interface with Ajax is one example.
- It's best if you can run old applications without changes while new ones are under development.
- The less time you can spend on temporary integration code, the better.
- If you need to serialize objects, try to serialize only the simplest possible objects, with only primitive attributes.

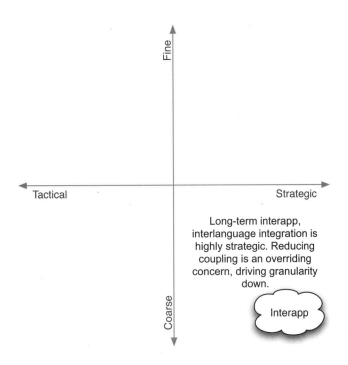

Figure 6.2: LONG-TERM INTERAPP, INTERLANGUAGE INTEGRATION DEMANDS A STRATEGIC VIEW

Interapplication Integration

In this scenario, you build each application in the best possible language, but each application is in its own language. You're betting that you can get extra productivity based on using the best possible language for each job, but you're limiting your integration costs and complexity by integrating only across major interfaces. For this strategy, careful planning is critical. You will want to do the following:

- Target applications to migrate.

- Define major application interfaces within these applications—interfaces that cross language boundaries.

- Assess the number, size, and granularity of requests that flow between applications. Cross-language interfaces are very expensive, and these items will all have a significant impact.

This strategy requires a strategic, coarse-grained view, as in Figure 6.2.

In the past, building distributed applications that talked across languages was a much more arduous process, but now, with SOA, this particular scenario is much easier to solve. Ruby in general and Ruby on Rails in particular have excellent integration with important SOA technologies.

Integrating with a Scripting Language

Integration can be a massive problem. Over time, the number of platforms and applications grows and will require some glue code to integrate things. Ruby is a great integration language for a variety of reasons:

- Ruby makes dealing with collections of objects easy. Files, databases, XML documents, and even formatted text are all collections. Ruby's language features such as regular expressions, closures, and ranges make it an excellent language for quickly translating data between formats.

- Ruby is terse and productive. Integration jobs often have short timelines. The target languages must therefore be productive and nimble. Ruby is both.

- Ruby values productivity over run-time efficiency. Since integration projects use low-level middleware (which is normally written in an efficient systems language like C or Java) to do most of the processing, run-time efficiency is less important.

In short, Ruby makes excellent glue code. As integration projects grew with Java, more and more people began to build applications from the ground up in Java, and integration became secondary. These are some examples of glue code that you might see between applications.

Data Munging

Enterprise applications often need to translate data from one format to another. For example, a shrink-wrapped sales application builds reports in XML format for delinquent accounts. A proprietary C application manages delinquent accounts but uses a proprietary interface and a proprietary file format. Ruby glue code can take the incoming XML code, parse it, and translate it into a form that the C application can understand.

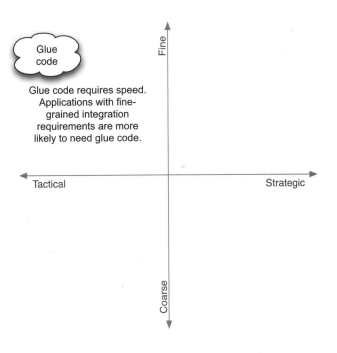

Figure 6.3: SPEED IS THE OVERRIDING CONCERN FOR GLUE CODE

Maintenance

Database applications often need maintenance. Free databases, such as PostgreSQL, or MySQL, may not have the tools to run this kind of maintenance on a periodic basis. But using the database API and a simple scheduled job (Unix operating systems use a feature called Cron to launch applications on a schedule), a Ruby script could run the scheduled backups and statistics and also build custom queries to build tables for reporting snapshots or the like.

Utilities

Enterprises often need quick utilities to solve targeted problems. For example, say your developers introduce a nasty bug, forgetting to set up some important data in the database, and causing applications to crash. Your support team could write a simple Ruby utility to fix the problem and run it, or have the user run it.

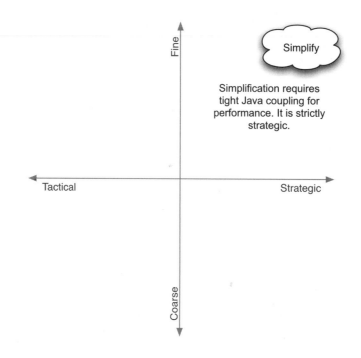

Figure 6.4: SIMPLIFICATION OF JAVA IS A STRATEGIC CONCERN REQUIR-
ING FINE-GRAINED INTEGRATION

Testing

Modern development places a much greater emphasis on automat-
ing testing. Fundamentally, testing is a scripting problem. Python and
Ruby both do exceptional jobs of testing. If test cases are easier to write
and run, your team will write more of them.

When you look at glue code, you're tying applications together that
may not integrate together cleanly on their own. As Figure 6.3, on the
preceding page, shows, glue code leans toward the tactical, fine-grained
interfaces. Bridges, middleware (like databases), and operating system
interfaces work well here.

Simplification

A much more ambitious plan is to build a single application that spans
multiple languages. If you're going to attack this additional level of complexity, you'll want a good reason to do so. The best reason to use Ruby

from within Java applications is simplification, as Thomas E. Enebo, project lead for JRuby, addresses below.

Java provides some core services that Ruby doesn't, and Ruby provides a much better programming language for some tasks. Web pages, business rules, testing code, configuration, and scripts are all much simpler in scripting languages. Right now, Java developers often reach for XML, a declarative language for data, when they'd be better off with a scripting language. In Figure 6.4, on the preceding page, you can see that the solutions lean heavily to fine-grained and strategic.

This strategy will gain increasing popularity as users begin to see the greater power of Ajax. End users are getting a taste of dynamic web sites with popular applications like Google Maps, and they are demanding more.

Java has never been a productive language for web development, so developers will increasingly look for ways to tie Java back ends to Ruby web development frameworks, including Ruby on Rails front ends, to take advantage of Ajax.

Just as Ruby can simplify some Java applications, you can use existing Java services to simplify Ruby applications. Ruby developers must often implement services Java developers take for granted, including JDBC, transaction libraries with two phase commit, and enterprise integration libraries. As JRuby matures, customers with existing infrastructure investments will be able to run Ruby and Java applications side by side.

Practical applications of JRuby—A discussion with Thomas E. Enebo

JRuby team lead

Q: What is JRuby?

JRuby is a Java implementation of the Ruby programming language. It boasts Java integration features. The first Java integration feature is the ability to reference and use Java classes from within the Ruby programming environment. This feature allows a user to write a Ruby program that could leverage a Java library. For example, let's say I need to work with an advanced XML capability called XML Schema, or some other unimplemented technology in Ruby, and I want to do this work in Ruby. Multiple XML Schema options exist in Java, but Ruby has no such library. JRuby can also adorn additional Ruby methods to a Java class making things more Ruby-like. Adding an each method and including Enumerable to Java.sql.ResultSet to make them more powerful would be an example of this.

The second Java integration feature is the ability to embed a Ruby interpreter in a Java application. Our primary vehicle for doing this is the Bean Shell Framework (BSF).

Ruby can be embedded via our internal APIs, too. I recently wrote a simple servlet that can pass requests off to Ruby scripts in a web container.

Q: Why is JRuby important to the Ruby community?

We now have another implementation of Ruby, and it will help solidify Ruby the language. Ruby has no formal specification.

Essentially, the implementation is the specification. Another implementation now exists. Over time JRuby will help root out ambiguities in the language over time whenever divergent behavior is spotted.

Ruby has not been ported to as many platforms as Java. JRuby runs on more platforms. Also, JRuby has long-term potential to pressure Ruby in areas that would otherwise likely go unchallenged. Native threading and tail recursion come to mind.

Java has a much larger user base than Ruby. JRuby adoption could grow Ruby's user base. One killer JRuby application could introduce a large number of Java programmers to Ruby.

Q: Why is JRuby important to the Java community?

More languages for the JVM will greatly strengthen Sun's position in their war with .NET. Additionally, JRuby provides a compelling dynamic typing option for the Java platform.

Embedding Ruby in a Java app provides a nice alternative to a pure statically typed solution. Ruby is a good tool for a Java programmer's toolbox.

The Java culture has not had anything disruptive happen in a while. Ruby on Java really could shake up people's preconceived notions of how programs must be written.

Java syntax is verbose and cumbersome. Even though it supports a limited idea of closures, it is almost painful to write one in Java syntax. Ruby syntax is much friendlier.

Q: What are people doing with JRuby today?

- Datavision. This is a reporting tool that embeds Ruby as its default reporting language. (See `http://datavision.sourceforge.net`)

- Spring with JRuby. Someone is working on a rapid prototyping system that uses JRuby and Spring. (For more details, see `http://thebogles.com/blog/2005/10/more-on-rapid-prototyping-using-jRuby-and-spring`)

- JEDIT and RDT. These two IDEs implement a Ruby integrated development environment. Both embed JRuby to parse and calculate positioning information of the Ruby abstract syntax tree (AST). RDT launches JRuby to provide information for debugging.

- Antbuilder. This effort is apparently inspired from Antbuilder in Groovy. (See `http://antbuilder.Rubyforge.org`)

- J2Rubee. Someone started working on a Ruby-based servlet. This one is a very new project, but it's promising. (See `http://j2rubee.sourceforge.net`)

- Testing frameworks. People are interested in using an embedded Ruby interpreter to generate test implementations of Java interfaces and pass them back to Java. This approach ends up yielding a simple syntactical way of writing Java test classes without Java (and class files).

Q: What projects would you attack today with JRuby?

I would build any one-off tool that you would normally write in Java. Let's say you want to write a database utility to update something for an application you are working on. You could just write it in Ruby. You would include the Java you need to use, like JDBC (the Java database integration class), and write your Ruby code to use the Java libraries directly.

I would also use Ruby as a configuration language. You could embed Ruby in a Java application and create a Ruby syntax vertical domain language. This approach gives you a nicer syntax for configuration with plenty of power.

I would consider making a servlet that embeds JRuby to provide an alternative to JSP for making simple apps in Ruby in a Java web container. I have personally thought about making a servlet/controller amenable to a ReST architectural style. And I think testing frameworks are a natural fit for JRuby.

Q: What projects would you not attack today?

We can't do the following:

- Anything low-latency or high-transaction. Charles Nutter has been working on reengineering the evaluation portion of our interpreter, but it is still not fast by many definitions. Once he has converted our interpreter to an iterative interpreter, we can consider a whole slew of optimizations not possible today, like making a Ruby byte code. We will also gain continuations and cheap exception handling.

- Anything using continuations. We do not support them yet.

- Anything that requires extending a Java class from Ruby and passing that back to a Java consumer. The Java consumer in this case will not see the changes. Extending an interface does work, however. This will be fixed by version 0.8.4.

Domain-Specific Languages

Often, developers provide applications that have embedded programming languages intended for application end users instead of programmers. Macros in Microsoft Office, formulas in a spreadsheet, and HTML documents in a web browser are a few examples. These languages work best when they use the terminology and syntax of the problem they seek to solve.

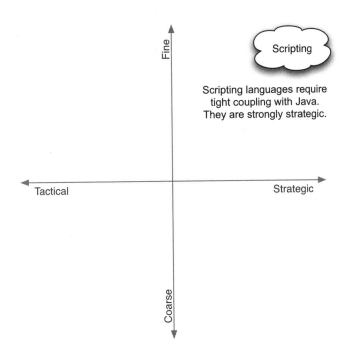

Figure 6.5: SIMPLIFICATION, LIKE SCRIPTING, REQUIRES VERY TIGHT COUPLING WITH JAVA AND IS STRONGLY STRATEGIC

Java does not provide a good syntax or vocabulary for most domain-specific languages. Extending Java to add the right vocabulary is also difficult. Java developers requiring a DSL must seek other options.

Ruby is particularly good at building DSL, and serves as a fine scripting language in its own right. Ruby on Rails makes excellent use of this capability.

The JRuby project makes it possible for you to build Java applications that use the Ruby language for scripting. Like simplification, this strategy is fine-grained and strategic (see Figure 6.5).

Supporting Technology

We'll categorize Java to Ruby technologies the same way we categorized strategies: coarse to fine and strategic to tactical. The pragmatic solutions, the Java to Ruby bridges, tend to provide spot integration, allowing a Ruby application to call a Java API through a specialized interface called a bridge.

These bridging technologies provide only primitive support for bridging the data types across languages and don't try to give you the best possible integration—they seek to be good enough.

The strategic solutions, such as web services and JRuby, provide a much more comprehensive solution, but they will require a steeper learning curve and possibly more complexity.

These are the major players.

- JRuby, an implementation of Ruby in the Java virtual machine.

- Java/Ruby bridges. Several bridges allow communication from Ruby to Java.

- SOAs. Ruby has several important web services technologies.

Coarse-grained technologies will provide a remote API, usually with web standards for transport with XML to describe messages. You get a relatively expensive but well-defined interface. If you don't have to use the interface too often, the performance overhead is not too bad. Fine-grained solutions such as JRuby and some of the bridges provide a much lower-level interface between Java and Ruby.

6.3 Ruby to Java Bridges

Over the last five years, a handful of Java to Ruby bridge solutions have emerged. Although the problems they solve are similar, the implementations are wildly different, and some have fallen out of favor. I'm going to list all of them here so you'll know which are under active development. at least at the time of this writing):

- *RJB, Ruby/Java Bridge.* This is a bridge that uses the Java Native Interface (JNI). Java's JNI is used primarily for C to Java integration, and it's a high-performance API. The performance is good, and the package is under active development. This bridge is more difficult to set up than some of the others, especially on alternate platforms such as Windows. But once it's set up, it's easy to use.

- *YAJB, Yet Another Java Bridge.* This bridge uses a common communication strategy called XML remote procedure calls. YAJB is very easy to install and configure. You don't need a C compiler to deploy it; you just drop the libraries into the right directory. This bridge is reasonably up-to-date, and seems to be actively maintained. There's an active mailing list. YAJB is a coarse, tactical tool.

- *RJNI, Ruby to Java Native Interface.* This bridge uses the Java Native Interface (JNI) to provide a Ruby to Java bridge with high-performance potential. It's not under active development, and goes only one way (for example, you can't do callbacks from Java, so rich user interface development is all but impossible).

  It was last updated more than a year ago, and it works only on Unix platforms, not Windows.

- *RJAVA.* This Ruby to Java bridge uses TCP/IP to communicate between Java and Ruby. It is not under active development and should not be used in production systems.

Advantages

As of this printing, the most prominent of these are YAJB (Yet Another Java Bridge) and RJB (Ruby to Java Bridge). The others are no longer being actively maintained (though that situation could well change). These types of tactical bridges have some definite advantages:

- *They are light.* They require only small libraries, and you can get them running relatively quickly (though the JNI versions have to be compiled).

- *They are simple to use.* The API for both of the major implementations is focused and easy to understand.

- *They are convenient.* You can easily cross boundaries with a simple method call.

Disadvantages

These technologies would both be quite useful in the tactical scenarios we discussed, such as small projects with targeted needs or for short-term scaffolding for larger projects. The bridges could be used for either coarse (YAJB) or fine (RJB) strategies. But they take a limited view of application architecture, so they're less than ideal for large-scale development across languages. These are the primary limitations:

- They don't seek to make transparent, bidirectional access between languages. You won't be able to build frameworks that have much bidirectional communication, such as plugging a Ruby business rule into a Java rules engine, for example.

- They don't seek broader integration to programming languages beyond Java or Ruby. Your interfaces will be usable only between Ruby and Java.

Of course, a typical bridge wouldn't seek to do all of those things. It's a tactical solution.

6.4 JRuby

JRuby, a project that's building a Ruby implementation in Java, is the most ambitious and active fine-grained Java to Ruby project. Today, the Ruby language is implemented in the C programming language. That trade-off makes Ruby fast but has behavior specific to its host operating system. Further, developers find extending Ruby more difficult because the basic building blocks are not all based on the same foundation— some are on Ruby, and some are on C. Charles O. Nutter talks about the status of Java to Ruby.

JRuby from the inside—A discussion with Charles O. Nutter

Core JRuby Developer

Q: What is JRuby?

JRuby is an implementation of the Ruby language on the Java platform. We generally consider it to be a Ruby virtual machine on top of the JVM. There are a number of VM features that Ruby requires that are not provided by the JVM, so we don't implement JRuby entirely with byte codes. Think of JRuby as a version of Ruby, written in Java.

Q: Why is JRuby important?

Ruby is fast becoming the language of choice for many types of applications, and not just web applications written in Rails. For example, we've also seen Ruby used to write system application servers and build tools like Rake. I personally would like to see JRuby used to implement business rules in a Java application, or web front-ends to Java services. JRuby also offers unique potential for running existing Ruby apps because the Java platform brings a full complement of APIs, frameworks, and services.

Java provides many features that the Ruby community doesn't have yet. Transaction management, JMS, JMX, remoting, and security—all of these enterprise services would be useful to a Ruby application.

For example, many users would like to use JDBC from Ruby on Rails, because so many database systems already have a JDBC driver written for them. We will eventually support running Rails in JRuby with JDBC, and provided a preview of this at JavaOne 2006. Swing is another good example. We've seen and demonstrated many scenarios where Swing apps could be implemented entirely in Ruby.

Ruby should be treated as another tool for implementing Java applications. The Java world is full of alternative languages: SQL, XML dialects, Velocity, Jelly (in Maven), JavaScript, web frameworks like JSP—the list goes on and on. There are dozens of alternative languages for the Java platform, and we think Ruby is one of the best. Sun has also announced their official support for making the Java platform multilingual. The upcoming release of Java SE 6 includes pluggability for scripting languages like Ruby, and will ship with a JavaScript interpreter.

JRuby can bring the powerful elegance of Ruby, its growing library of frameworks and applications, and its large and dedicated community to the Java platform.

Q: What are people doing with JRuby today?

People are already doing automated testing, writing unit tests in Ruby and using JRuby to exercise their systems. We've also seen Java-based reporting software with Ruby as a report language. A few developers have been implementing Swing applications in JRuby as well. Our big focus recently has been on running existing Ruby applications like IRB (which works now) and Ruby on Rails (which works for simple apps), so people have also started using JRuby to simply run Ruby applications.

Q: Where does JRuby break down?

Right now, we're passing 80 to 85% of the core Ruby test cases. *(Editor's note: the Ruby language has a full automated test suite that exercises much of the Ruby language.)* We are working to get as close to 100% as possible, but we'll never get all of the way there. We'll never be able to support operating system–specific calls, and we can't do native C calls in Java. We should be able to pass over a high percentage of the test cases, though, and we already have many large and complicated Ruby applications working without those unsupported features.

Q: Where is JRuby going in the immediate future?

Right now, we are undergoing a core redesign. We are working toward a stackless model to support continuations and more flexible threading models. We want to be able to exactly match the way Ruby handles continuations and threads in JRuby.

We would like to take greater advantage of Rake. I think it could potentially replace Ant scripts in the future. We have working prototypes of servlets for running run Ruby web applications, and we made use of this for our Rails presentation at JavaOne. In production mode, the performance was quite acceptable.

I would like to have the JRuby VM redesigned by the second or third quarter of 2006. I want us to support major features of Ruby that we're missing, especially thread scheduling and continuations. I would like to have just-in-time compilation. I am also working on compilation options for JRuby. There's great potential for improving performance with just-in-time and ahead-of-time compilation. Performance will always be a priority. We'll always work to improve performance.

We continue to work toward supporting as many major Ruby applications as possible. IRB works now, Rake mostly works, Rails is coming along quickly, and RubyGems is just around the corner. Running existing Ruby apps is one of the most compelling scenarios for JRuby, since as Rails has shown, Ruby offers new and unique ways to write software.

Q: What is the significance of running Ruby on Rails in JRuby at JavaOne 2006?

Successfully running a simple Rails app under JRuby means there's a giant new opportunity for deployment and integration of Rails in existing enterprises. Current Java shops will soon be able to deploy Rails apps side-by-side with standard Java web and enterprise applications, making use of existing infrastructure and services. All the features of the Java platform will be available to Rails apps, and the agile development model of Rails will empower Java developers.

I'm very excited to start deploying my own Rails apps under JRuby.

The Java virtual machine is the environment that runs all Java applications. If you were to build your language on top of the JVM, you could run anywhere that Java does, and you could take advantage of Java services such as the database interface (JDBC), security, distributed transactions, and servlets. The JVM is portable, fast, reliable, and secure. Many managers have a comfort zone with the Java platform that they've never experienced with another language. As we saw in the interview, JRuby is a Ruby virtual machine, written in Ruby, that runs in the Java virtual machine. JRuby is more than a stand-alone Ruby implementation, though. It also seeks to integrate Java and Ruby at unprecedented levels. With JRuby, you'll be able to do the following:

- Call a Java object from Ruby, as if it were a Ruby object.

- Use Java frameworks from within the Ruby langauge.

- Let Ruby take advantage of some of the JVM's strengths.

Developers who work on the Ruby language rely on automated tests that run whenever anyone changes Ruby. The JRuby implementation today passes around 85% of those test cases for the base Ruby language, so you can already do some impressive things with JRuby.

Practical Uses

You've now seen the major JRuby features and interviews of two of the primary project leads. With this information, we can begin to identify the practical uses of JRuby today and in the near future. As the Thomas Enebo interview on page 103 describes, these areas seem particularly inviting:

- *Testing.* Automated testing is catching on in many Java communities, but the testing capabilities of Java pale in comparison to

Other Cross-Language Projects

The question is this: how ambitious is JRuby, and has this kind of integration been pulled off in the past? If you want to see examples of this kind of integration in the past, look at attempts to build programming languages on a common foundation. Here are some projects that I've seen:

- Microsoft's .NET environment is perhaps the most interesting movement to integrate several languages under one umbrella. They have Visual Basic, C++, C, and C# all unified under one operating environment, called the CLR (*common language runtime*). Now, more than 25 languages exist for the CLR. The Mono project is an open source implementation of Microsoft's CLR. So far, the project has not been able to keep up with Microsoft's changes, and adoption has been limited. With the Novell acquisition, Mono is beginning to pick up adoption and gain credibility.
- Java's C++ integration never achieved broad success. In fact, the adoption of JNI (the Java Native Interface), has been sporadic at best.
- IBM's System Object Model (SOM) was to serve as a foundation for object-oriented languages in the early 1990s. They succeeded in building support under C and C++, but interpreted and dynamic languages bogged them down. After investing hundreds of thousands into DSOM (Distributed SOM) and a product called Component Broker, they eventually abandoned the effort in favor of WebSphere.
- IBM's VisualAge project actually succeeded in building a common foundation underneath both Smalltalk and Java. The Java version of the tool actually ran on the same virtual machine as the Smalltalk version of the tool. Still, IBM never was able to keep up with revisions in the JVM, and Visual Age was eventually abandoned in favor of Eclipse.

Java never achieved fine-grained, generic integration with C++, but Microsoft seems to have had limited success, and with close to infinite resources. Still, you have to acknowledge that there are already dozens of languages on the JVM such as Jython (a port of Python), REXX, Lisp, and some experimental languages called Groovy, P-Nuts, and Nice. Most of those implementations were open source language, like JRuby.

Ruby's. Java and Ruby expert Stuart Halloway says a dynamic language changes the way you think as you test, by enabling more possibilities.

- *Simplifying.* When you or your customers need to write many small scripts, that's a hint that Java may not be the best possible solution. Business rules, web pages, test cases, build scripts, and configuration are just a few examples.

- *Extending Ruby.* Java has many additional utilities and capabilities that Ruby lacks. JRuby can give you those capabilities.

- *Extending Java.* Ruby makes an excellent domain-specific language.

Looking Forward

In the near future, if JRuby development continues to improve, the scenarios will open up rapidly. The possibilities are endless, but the JRuby team seems most passionate about these:

- *Running Ruby code from within a Java servlet.* This approach gives Ruby programmers access to the most robust web servers in the world and gives Java programmers access to a better templating language.

- *Using Ruby on Rails for the user interface and existing Java legacy code as the model.* This level of integration would open up a whole new world of productivity and rapid web development capabilities to Java developers.

We've just scratched the surface here. Keep in mind that today, JRuby is under heavy development, and would be an aggressive move to try and deploy it now. If you want to use it, make sure to stay well within the realm of the recommended uses. This said, the future of JRuby seems to be bright.

6.5 Service-Oriented Architectures

In the last five years, we've seen an increasing movement toward an idea of SOA. At its simplest form an SOA has services and consumers. The goal is to reuse major services and loosen the coupling between the service provider and the consumer. That's a pretty broad definition, but commercial implementations of SOA use a few common patterns. An SOA should do the following:

- Use common standards for sending messages and formatting message content. Internet standards drive communications; Web services standards deliver messages; and XML represents data.

- Keep interfaces simple. Provide complexity through message content. Practically, this means you'll use a few messaging methods to send and deliver messages. The messages, implemented in XML, can be as simple or complex as your applications need them to be.

- Expose coarse-grained interfaces. XML and remote messaging are both expensive, so minimizing them through a coarse strategy makes sense.

Now, we're starting to describe web services as you see them implemented today. So, let's create a more practical definition of an SOA. Service-oriented architecture is an architectural style that

- decouples consumers and service providers by providing a common set of well-defined interfaces,

- exposes these interfaces through some form of web services for messaging, and

- structures message payload with XML.

As you can well imagine, SOA can take many vastly different forms. We're going to focus on the small scale: how do you build a Ruby application that can share its services with other languages and consume services from Java applications? To do so, we'll focus on a simple form of web services.

SOA and web services need standards and conventions to be useful. These standards serve as a communications backbone, define a higher-level messaging protocol, and structure the payload of messages.

Internet

Web services build on top of basic Internet standards. The Internet starts with TCP and IP, which provide the communication protocol and define the addressing scheme that you use today. The dots, numbers, and names you see in your browser address bar all represent addresses organized in a giant tree.

HTML is the language that represents web pages. HTTP defines the way we move documents on the Web. Going to a website uses HTTP to get a document. Clicking the submit button on a form sends the contents of the form back to the server. Several other standards, like HTTPS for security, sit on top of these basic standards. Ruby has excellent support for these Internet standards through core libraries.

XML

HTML is adequate for presenting documents, but it does not do a good job of representing documents. For example, if you're reading a catalog on a web page, you can tell that there's a price, but computers can't. There's nothing in the document that ties the data $14.95 to a price for a CD, or any price at all, for that matter. Enter XML. XML is a language for expressing data. You could have a document with <price>14.95</price>. And you'd know the meaning of the data.

Web services make broad use of XML. Most importantly, some web services use XML to communicate the structure of messages, and almost all kinds of web services use XML to communicate the structure of the message payload.

To understand Ruby's support for XML, you need a brief history. In the beginning, XML was simple and elegant. XML use grew rapidly, and people began to press it into use in more and broader places. As time went on, controlling vendors changed XML to accommodate the most extreme customers. Changes like XML Schema and XML Namespaces complicated XML tremendously. Many developers tend to ignore those extensions.

Ruby supports several good XML processors. REXML is the most prominent, and its use in Ruby on Rails will increase its acceptance and penetration in the Ruby community. The Ruby community tends to value simplicity. Perhaps it's not too surprising that Ruby has excellent support for base XML, but support for extensions such as Schema is not as readily available. (The support for XML extensions will doubtlessly grow, though.)

Ruby also supports a simplified data representation called YAML, which bizarrely stands for YAML Ain't a Markup Language. Frameworks like Ruby on Rails use YAML when XML seems too complicated for the job.

SOAP-Based Web Services

The web services history is similar to the XML history: you can choose between heavyweight and lightweight implementations, and the Ruby community embraces the lightweight version first. In the early hype-filled years for web services, IBM and Microsoft controlled major standards and fueled much of the development. They defined a stack of APIs based on an XML-based messaging scheme over the Internet, called SOAP, and built on that stack over time. Ironically, SOAP originally stood for Simple Object Access Protocol. Early web services based on a thin wrapper around SOAP had a simple elegance about them, but now, there's nothing simple about the SOAP-based web services stack.

This kind of web service is now incredibly complex and increasingly dependent on tools and libraries in Java and .NET for any hope of effective use. Widespread integration beyond these languages is a pipe dream. Ruby does support SOAP through several APIs, if you need to go down that route. The problem is that the web services stack of interfaces is so tall and high and complex that it has become practically useless to languages that aren't the center of the known universe. Enter ReST.

ReST-Based Web Services

Some observant developers noticed that the Web has been used for years to deliver services, and the Web's version of web services didn't look much like the tower of SOAP. Roy Fielding[1] did some research on the Web's behavior and coined the term ReST (Representational State Transfer) to describe web services as they existed "in the wild."

Instead of starting with a message like the SOAP-based web services (or a doomed architecture known as CORBA), ReST starts with resources on the Web. Messages simply create, read, update, and delete resource items. ReST-based web services rely strictly on TCP/IP and HTTP to move XML documents and on a thin API on top of both.

Ruby provides excellent support for ReST, merely adequate support for SOAP, and more limited support for full SOAP-based web services. Rails, in particular, is a fantastic example of the simplicity of ReST.

---

[1]http://www.w3.org/2001/tag/webarch/

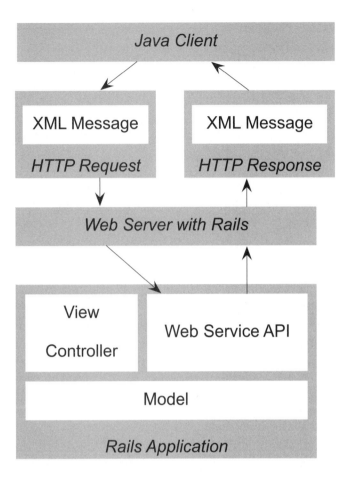

Figure 6.6: RAILS USES A REST STYLE OF WEB SERVICE

Putting Web Services into Practice

Now that you know what standards Ruby supports, we can talk about implementing a coarse-grained, strategic integration strategy. We will focus on a strategy implemented in Rails, but you can easily use the similar frameworks to achieve the same result.

Figure 6.6, shows the overall application architecture. Your base application will have layers for model, view, and controller. Both your web services layer and your controllers will share the model. Other applications will communicate to this application layer with simple CRUD methods.

Let's drill down. A client, written in some arbitrary language, sends a message over HTTP. We know it's going to be a request to create, read, update, or delete a document. The incoming request will specify any needed document (like an input form) in XML. This request comes into Ruby through a Ruby-enabled web server, and Rails routes the request to the API layer. The API layer uses REXML to parse the request, and the Rails model logic does the work. Then, the REXML layer sends an XML document back as a response to the request, if necessary.

If this flow seems familiar to you, it should. This flow represents the way the Web has worked for decades. The model has proven to be simple, scalable, and extensible. It fueled the e-commerce explosion that powered the growth of the Web throughout the late 1990s.

The Possibilities

You can use this style of application development on both the Java side and the Ruby side. All your applications will have layers accessible by either your private views or your external applications. It's a compelling vision that works in a variety of circumstances:

- *Across languages.* Since documents are in XML and flow across Internet standards, you need support only for these simple standards to make ReST-based web services work. With Java, that means you need support for servlets, HTTP, and XML.
- *Within a multilanguage application.* If your application consists of major, coarse-grained layers (such as the business logic and user interface for a web application), you could pick the best language for each part of the application. JRuby may soon enable a Rails front end against a Spring and Hibernate back end.
- *Across applications.* This strategy works across applications easily. You can call other languages that have a similar web services implementation, and other applications can access your model.
- *With legacy applications.* You can access legacy applications by using glue code. You'd access the legacy application with a tactical bridge technology (such as the C interface or one of the Java-Ruby bridges) and then add the web services layer to your glue code.
- *For scalability.* The approach can scale the same way that the Web scales. For a higher-traffic implementation, you can just let your existing networking infrastructure do your load balancing, because this shared-nothing architecture works the same way that many websites work.

But you can appreciate the importance of planning. The more applications that share this style of service, the more services that can participate in the overall vision. But even if you decide to implement web services, dramatically different implementations from site to site will complicate your integration and force you to use more glue code.

That completes our review of your technical Java to Ruby integration options. In this chapter, we looked at the difficult technical integration problems. In the next chapter, we'll look into the political challenges of ramping up.

6.6 Executive Summary

- Ruby provides excellent integration options for many languages, including Java.

- Options range from tactical to strategic and from fine to coarse.

- JRuby is rapidly maturing and is a Ruby implementation on the JVM.

- Java to Ruby bridges are more tactical, allowing Ruby code to call specifically designed function points in Java.

- Web services allow a coarse-grained, strategic integration.

- Ruby frameworks favor simplified implementations of XML and web services.

Unless you try to do something beyond what you have already mastered, you will never grow.
 ▶ Ralph Waldo Emerson

Chapter 7

Ramping Up

Success can be a dangerous thing. Succeeding with a pilot is challenging, even when you have a good technology on your side. After you've done some initial groundwork, you'll want to grow. Replicating your early success can be tougher than you think. In this chapter, we'll look at the ways you can begin to extend your success into the mainstream. To do so, you're going to have to deal with a growing staff and issues related to a broader deployment.

To be perfectly frank, we don't have a whole lot of experience to draw from when deploying Ruby. Although it's becoming clear that more people will increasingly depend on Ruby in the near future, few shops have large development efforts underway. Still, we do have some experience with Ruby-like languages. Many enterprises use Perl, which has deployment strategies and performance characteristics similar to Ruby. Smalltalk has been used in production in conservative Wall Street firms for more than 30 years now, and the language and application architectures tend to be similar. So by looking at development with similar languages, you can intelligently build a strategy for ramping up.

7.1 Building Your Staff

The first order of business will be expanding your talent pool. Since you can't simply rely on dozens of offshore organizations, your local Java user group, or an available pool of tens of thousands of Java developers, you'll have to be a little more creative. Despite the market realities, you can grow your Ruby skills and grow them quickly. Before you begin to despair, consider the factors that mitigate the smaller pool of Ruby talent:

- Since Ruby is such an attractive technology, you'll find these kinds of positions easier to fill. Developers want Ruby jobs. They'll also often work for less.

- Ruby developers can do more work than Java developers. Numbers vary, but I've generally used one-third to one-fifth of the required Java developers for a typical project.

- Since projects are smaller, your mentors go further. And since the language has integrated frameworks instead of dozens of sprawling choices, you can settle on a framework and educate Ruby developers much more quickly than Java developers. That means you can build teams faster with Ruby.

- The nature of an emerging language and the absence of certification programs means there is less of an assembly-line feel to the community. I've found that so far, Ruby developers on average are better than their Java counterparts.

So although you might need to stretch to fill out a medium-sized organization, you can fill your positions. And you should have no problem whatsoever building a smaller project team. Let's look at recruiting strategies you can use.

Recruiting Strategies

In some geographies, you won't have recruiting problems at all. In Austin, the Ruby on Rails user group has more than 30 active members. Other Ruby user groups are much larger. But let's just assume that you're not lucky enough to have dozens of Ruby developers close by, and you need to work harder. You will have to expand your search using one of a few strategies:

- Train your internal developers. You can build good Ruby developers from good Java developers. Good programmers know how to learn.

- Build on a dynamic foundation. Developers who know languages similar to Ruby, like Perl and Smalltalk, can learn Ruby quickly.

- Engage the Ruby communities. Find local user groups. Post jobs on the active Ruby newsgroups. Austin, Columbus, Salt Lake City, and St. Louis all have active Ruby user groups.

- Shift to a top-heavy strategy. Rather than trying to find four low-cost programmers, hire one top-grade one.

- Hire short-term help. You can hire short-term contractors, or look for contract-to-hire help.

- Consider hiring a remote developer. Tools to manage remote development are getting much better and making remote work easier. Rails, in particular, is easy to manage with geographic distribution. (Rails itself was built this way.)

All things being equal, you want small numbers of great programmers rather than large numbers of mediocre programmers. A great Ruby programmer will get much more leverage than three or four average Java programmers who are just learning Ruby.

Targeting Languages

I've taught Ruby to several different classes of programmers and seen others in classroom situations. In every case, good programmers can learn to be productive with Ruby quickly. Learning the intricacies of techniques like metaprogramming can take a little more time.

These are some experiences that I've had with the ramp-up time for other languages. As you'd expect, the more similar the language, the quicker the ramp-up. Perl, Python, Lisp, and Smalltalk developers can be particularly successful.

Among the first-tier choices are languages that match Ruby, in syntax, in the abstract, or in design patterns:

- *Smalltalk.* Ruby is very close to Smalltalk. Both are dynamically-typed and object oriented, and many of the patterns that work well in Smalltalk (for example, features such as code blocks and method chaining) also work well in Ruby.

- *Lisp.* In general, programmers who are comfortable with Lisp generally adapt to other languages very well. Ruby makes a good platform for Lisp developers, because Ruby has many Lisp-like features. Lisp is in a family of functional languages, and many Ruby features can be used in a functional way.

- *Python.* Developers who have used Python also usually work well with Ruby. Python syntax is relatively close to Ruby's, and the type systems are similar.

- *Perl.* The Ruby language has many features of Perl. Programmers tend to be creative and very productive.

Be careful, though. Programming hygiene is important to your ability to maintain a program long-term. Get someone who has done full object-oriented application development rather than a few Perl operating system shell scripts.

Second-tier choices on a résumé include developers who may not be application developers or developers in object-oriented languages with less in common to Ruby:

- *Java.* There are many Java developers out there with vastly different skills. Not all are what they claim to be. Some Java developers are highly dependent on their tools and will struggle without them. Most Java developers who are comfortable with command-line development and dynamic Java features such as reflection and aspect-oriented programming can learn the basics quickly. Getting the intricacies of testing, metaprogramming, and dynamic languages can take a little more time for the casual Java developer.

- *C#.* This language today is similar to Java. They are both statically typed, compiled, and highly dependent on tools. C# programmers tend to lean on their tools a little harder than others.

- *C++.* This language is strictly compiled and very difficult to learn. C++ developers who have done it for a while must be very competent. Still, C++ is not nearly as dynamic or as high level as Ruby.

These languages are poor fits, because they are so different from Ruby:

- *COBOL, FORTRAN, Pascal, etc.* Developers of procedural versions of these languages often need to make a big transition in two ways. First, those developers must learn the whole new object-oriented programming paradigm. Second, they must learn techniques that make dynamic languages so productive. Often, they need to learn web standards as well.

If you have time, you don't *have* to get an experienced Ruby programmer in order to successfully build applications. With a little training, you'll be able to ramp up a team quickly.

The Recruiting Process

The recruiting process is not much different from recruiting any candidate. You'll just allocate your resources a little differently and use different strategies to screen candidates. Here are the steps of a typical recruiting process:

1. Reach your intended pool.
2. Trim your list.
3. Interview your candidates.
4. Close your candidates.

The primary differences in your process will be the first and second steps. You'll use different strategies to reach your talent pool, because the Ruby community is smaller. You'll also trim your list less aggressively, because you'll have fewer candidates.

As you define your initial candidate list, you'll want to use the Ruby community. Ruby user groups are growing rapidly, so don't neglect that angle. You may also expand your search using some of the techniques mentioned in the previous section, such as expanding to different languages or geographies.

When it's time to trim your list, you'll want to lean harder on phone screens than résumé content, because phone screens are more effective at determining qualified candidates. Then, you can move into the formal interview process as usual. Here are a couple of thoughts to keep in mind:

- Require a coding test! Programmers should program before you give them a job. You want to be building on top of an effective foundation.

- If you don't have the skill to make good hiring decisions, get help. It's easy to enlist help on interview day from consultants to grade coding tests, do phone screens, or even be part of a technical interview. All of these tasks can be handled remotely, at quite reasonable rates.

7.2 Building Skills Internally

In all of the strategies we mentioned, your basic goal is to expand your talent pool. But you can't compromise quality. You need to make sure your candidates are technically strong, have rock-solid work ethics, and are good fits.

With a strong internal staff and a little time, you shouldn't have to gamble on work ethic and cultural fit. You can just build your skills internally, augmenting only with full-time or temporary mentors. Strong developers with desire can make the transition. Most will love Ruby. When you build skills internally, you send a message to your developers that you're willing to invest in them. Loyalty cuts both ways.

- Consider making at least one hire of a senior developer, either short-term or long-term. The hire may seem expensive but will pay for itself quickly through the productivity of your overall team.

- Classroom study is important. The classroom context is best for learning broadly what is possible.

- Mentoring helps. Developers who have role models will learn faster and make fewer critical errors.

- Share your code base. If everyone can work on all the files when it's time, you'll reduce the risk that bad or incorrect code will go unnoticed.

Though Ruby education will be much quicker than Java education (I mentioned earlier that my typical training for a Java developer takes at least four times as long as training for a similar Ruby developer), keep in mind that building skills still takes time. Your developers will need to use the tools, preferably under the direction of a senior developer, to advance their skills quickly.

Training senior-level developers internally takes time. ThoughtWorks builds the skills for their staff through an extensive training program that takes months, but they get much better productivity over the lifetime of their consultants and better retention with this strategy. Longer-term goals will give you the option of building skills internally.

Education

With a language like Java, you can pick from a wide variety of classes from hundreds of vendors. IBM shops can just pick up the phone and arrange a custom course. Ruby courses are not as widely available, though you can increasingly find courses from many reputable firms. If you go with someone who has less of a track record or reputation, here are some ideas that you should target in a course:

- Try to keep classes short. It's hard to focus for a whole week, and it's even harder to apply what you've learned over that period of time. You'll have much better success if you break up longer courses into several two- to three-day segments.

- Use instructors with real Rails programming experience. Practical experience means everything in this arena, since the language is new. Some trainers will try to break into the field without practical experience, and they will likely miss important topics that can save a typical developer a tremendous amount of time, or worse, teach techniques that are not secure or sound.

- Make sure the course has adequate lab time. Some instructors will ask your team to bring their own laptops and install required software. This approach is ideal, because it allows you to keep your programming exercises that you've worked on yourself and makes the attendees build a working environment.

Ruby on Rails training is ramping up sharply. A list of educators and classes is available online.[1]

Mentoring

Classroom training is no substitute for effective mentoring. You can use several strategies to mentor your staff, especially in the early stages:

- *Pair programming.* Pair programming is the most intense mentoring possible. A mentor can give much more intense instruction through pair programming.
- *Proximity.* Place all programmers in an open seating arrangement (often called a *bull pen*) without walls. Your goal is to get questions answered quickly, when quick answers matter most.
- *Electronic proximity.* A motivated team can communicate well with electronic tools. Skype is one of my favorites, because I can maintain three or four running chats with pupils without disrupting my flow too much and still pick up the phone when it's appropriate.
- *Gatekeeper model.* A mentor looks over all new code that's checked into a project. This way, a mentor can make sure that the best Ruby coding techniques apply to a given problem.

One of the most often overlooked keys to rapid learning is to keep your developers from getting stuck for long periods of time. Although some degree of problem solving is a healthy and necessary experience, long periods of fixing small problems frustrates developers and kills motivation to code and learn. Having an experienced programmer available to remove roadblocks is critical.

---

[1]http://rubyonrailsworkshops.com/

As you make mentoring possible, don't forget the needs of your mentors. Mixing teaching with development is much more demanding than simple development. If you expect programmers to mentor as they code, count on less productivity for that developer. If you set project schedules that don't allow much time, it's the mentoring that ultimately will suffer the most.

7.3 Short-Term Augmentation

Many development managers would like to build all their software internally. Consultants and contractors, especially those with skill, can be prohibitively expensive. Although long-term consultants and contract labor may not always be cost-effective, you can get your money's worth by using short-term help carefully, especially at ramp-up time.

The key to effectively using consultants is to look for ways to multiply the impact of your dollars. Jump-starts leverage talent to educate while delivering an application. Design reviews seek to involve help in the early stages when mistakes are the most costly and research is the most demanding. Recruiting seeks to tap the experience of consultants to screen and interview candidates. Each of these techniques requires only short-term investment but has long-lasting consequences.

Jump-Starts

Sometimes, it makes sense to send off whole projects to a third party for turnkey development, but if you're going to make a long-term commitment to Ruby, you'd often be better off working alongside a consultant. You're looking for a jump-start.

The goal of a jump-start is to ramp up a development team quickly while building a production application. You can call the jump-start successful only if you do both. A typical jump-start package will include everything you need to get a project running quickly, ensuring plenty of learning opportunities for your staff. When you enlist jump-start services, you'll want to consider the following:

- *Some classroom training.* This will give your developers a broad perspective of what they can expect from Ruby.

- *A planning phase.* Letting your regular developers and the jump-start team participate in the same training exercise will ensure that the consultants follow your process or that you'll be able to pick up any process introduced by the consultant when she goes home.

- *A development phase.* You should make sure that your developers have enough access to the consultant and that you keep your developers as free as possible from old projects to immerse themselves in the new language. (It's harder to learn a new language if you have to keep using an old one for, say, maintenance.)

- *An integrated automated testing strategy.* Any dynamic language should use automated tests to catch bugs that would normally be caught by a compiler.

- *A post-deployment support plan.* The project should include some support, post-deployment, for a period of time after the project goes into production to make sure you have expert help available should critical issues emerge.

A jump-start combines short-term training, with a chance for your developers to pair program with a recognized expert. You also get the long-term value of a working application, built by an expert.

Turnkey

You can certainly hire someone to build a turnkey application in Ruby, and you can build cost-effective solutions without having to go offshore. Ruby can give you the advantage of rapid turnaround, which would allow more regular demonstrations. For any complex system, user feedback is critical. But technology is only a small part of the problem. People, and their decisions, will determine the success or failure of your overall system. So if you have a choice, don't shop for a Ruby solution. Shop for a solution, and hire the best possible team. Then, let them build your systems.

Design Reviews

My favorite way to use consultants is the design review. In these short, focused encounters, your goal is to learn as much about a project as you can. You should employ experts in the field, and you should ask for some kind of record of the review. The outcome should be an assessment of the project and what should be done. You can use design reviews at any stage of development, but for a new language, they will be particularly effective at the beginning of a starting project. You'll look to accomplish one or more of these tasks:

- *Fit.* An expert can help you assess the fit of Ruby for a particular project. For this type of engagement, you'll want someone with experience in both languages, presumably Java and Ruby.

- *Process.* Development with Ruby will be far different from Java, and you can get maximum advantage if you're able to tailor your process. Automated testing becomes more important, and you can get feedback from users more often.

- *Sizing.* Development projects on new technologies are hard to size, because you don't have accumulated experience.

- *High-level design.* A good consultant with experience can help you choose the right approaches to major problems and suggest the architecture of the major layers of the system. He can also discuss your network design or hosting options.

- *Deployment strategy.* Having someone who has deployed Ruby before can help you take advantage of the capabilities of the platform and avoid pitfalls.

By employing a design review, you hope to mitigate risk by tapping the experience of someone who has done it before. Short engagements are a productive, cost-effective way to mitigate risk and learn about holes in your current plans before they can bite you. When you're choosing, do what you would normally do. Value experience over other credentials, check your references, and prefer referrals over someone you don't know.

7.4 Preparing the Way

Conservative organizations may need to wait until there's more momentum before beginning a wholesale migration. Others might be starting Java projects today that cannot be changed. Still, even if you're not quite ready to make a wholesale move to Ruby, you can still prepare the way for a future migration by some careful investments. Adopting friendly conventions, subtle changes in your hiring practices, and some changes in architecture will go a long way toward providing a smoother migration.

Conventions

Most people who adopt Ruby today are planning on using Ruby on Rails. The database layer, Active Record, is much easier to map to Ruby if you follow some naming conventions. Most of the naming conventions won't lock you into Rails. They just make good sense. These are the highlights:

- Tables should have names that are English plurals. For example, the people database holds person objects.

- Use object identifiers named id. Databases use columns to identify a row in the database. For example, a Social Security number could identify a person in a database. Object-oriented specialists like to introduce identifiers with no real-world business value.

- Foreign keys should be named object_id. Database systems use foreign keys to relate two tables. In Active Record, a row named person_id would point to a row in the people database.

- Join tables should use the names of the tables they join. Database systems use join tables to relate two tables. For example, a table relating professors to a given workshop would have a table called professors_workshops.

If you're able to follow these conventions, your Active Record objects will require much less code. A few other naming conventions will matter, such as Ruby's notion of inheritance, but if you follow these rules, you'll be most of the way there.

Architecture

As you're preparing old applications for Ruby integration or enabling older ones for longer-term integration, you can follow some simple guidelines to ease your transition:

- *MVC separation.* If you design your Java applications with the idea that views are just services that use models, you'll be able to quickly wrap that model with a service-oriented architecture and consume those services with Ruby user interfaces.

- *SOA.* Java developers are beginning to use service-oriented architectures. If you build your back-end logic in a certain way, you'll be able to consume those services with many different applications. SOA layers, more than any other philosophy, make it easy to consume services across languages.

- *ReST-based web services.* You saw in the previous chapter that both Java and .NET platforms tend to use one of two strategies for web services: ReST and Microsoft/IBM style. By far the simplest to implement is ReST style, and Rails provides excellent integration.

- *Shared-nothing architecture.* There are many strategies for achieving scalability. You've seen that the strategy for LAMP-based solutions is a shared-nothing architecture. If you code your Java applications that way, you'll find that your network infrastructure will be very similar across programming languages.

- *HTML and JavaScript on the client.* Some Java frameworks like Spring's web MVC and Tapestry rely less on Java-specific components like JSP (JavaServer Pages) and JSTL (Java Standard Tag Library) tags. The more that you can rely on portable technologies like HTML and JavaScript, the better. Some JavaScript frameworks that enable things like Ajax work with Java and Ruby projects.

- *Standards supported by Ruby when you build your applications.* For example, you'll want to make sure that a version of Ruby XML supports a particular XML feature before you use it on the Java side.

These are just some of the things that you can do within your Java project to ease your transition to Ruby. This list is not exhaustive, and it's likely to change. If you plan to move to Ruby tomorrow, learn enough about Ruby to prepare for it today.

7.5 A Brief Word about Deployment

When you build a small proof-of-concept application, deployment is not necessarily a huge issue when you push it into production for the first time. Deploying a mission-critical application with a broad footprint, thousands of files, and expectations of a ten-year life span is a completely different story. You'll want to get your deployment story straight. The good news is that excellent solutions exist. Your goal for deployment should be threefold:

- Deployment should be completely automated. Don't create opportunities for user-introduced mistakes.

- Deployment should be recoverable. You should be able to back up to the previous release.

- Deployment should manage important dependencies. You need to be able to manage database changes in an automated way as well.

You should know about a few technologies that will help you with deployment. I'll stick with Ruby on Rails, but these techniques and technologies can work across many Ruby projects.

Capistrano

37signals, the company that brought you Ruby on Rails, offers Capistrano, previously named SwitchTower. It's a utility that will let you deploy your application to a remote server. It works best for web applications written in Ruby on Rails but can be extended to easily work with other technologies as well. Here are the core capabilities:

- You can deploy applications with a single command.

- You can roll back a deployment to the previous state with one command.

- Capistrano can issue parallel commands for deployment tasks that must reach across multiple servers.

- Capistrano can check your code out of a repository, which is Subversion by default.

Best of all, it's an open source tool with commercial backing and wide use. Working with these technologies will help you build a strong foundation for your deployments. In the sidebar, Jamis Buck discusses his evolution and use of Capistrano. 37signals deploys directly from development to production, but Capistrano can deploy to staging environments as well. I would expect many shops to use staging environments instead.

Deploying Ruby—A discussion with Jamis Buck interview

37signals

Q: You work with the applications for some of the largest Rails applications in the world. What are the most important factors to consider when deploying software?

Zero downtime is the biggest thing. We need to be able to push updates without inconveniencing our customers whenever possible. Naturally, some upgrades will require that we take our applications offline for a period of time (like when we are making DB schema changes and such), but for the vast majority of our updates all we are doing is pushing an update to the code or views.

Q: What are the most important features of a deployment system?

Zero downtime, as I mentioned, is pretty critical. It is also very important that deployments occur atomically so that visitors don't see a bizarre mixture of "old app" and "new app" during the deployment. This atomic deployment must occur in parallel across multiple machines, as well. We need to be able to painlessly and quickly push new releases and just as easily back out of a bad release. And for those rare deployments where we need to take our applications offline for an hour, we also need to be able to tell visitors that the application is down for maintenance and to prevent access to the application during that period.

Q: How do you manage deployment at 37signals?

With Capistrano (http://manuals.rubyonrails.com/read/book/17). We used to do it all by hand, back when we had a single application (Basecamp) and it ran on a single machine. Now, however, we have four applications, and a cluster of servers that we deploy to, and trying to do that consistently and atomically by hand would be excruciating. I wrote Capistrano to remove that pain. Deploying Basecamp, for instance, is as simple as typing "rake deploy".

As I mentioned, we don't have an intermediate staging environment like many shops do. When we need to push a bug fix or release a new feature, we first make sure it is well tested (as defined primarily by our unit tests) in our development environment, and then we deploy it directly to production. This works for us primarily because we are a small shop and the amount of coordination needed to make sure everything is safe for deployment is minimal. However, Capistrano is reportedly working very well for people who do use a staging environment, so if we ever need that feature, it's going to be a no-brainer to add it to our process.

> **Q: What's the relationship between Capistrano and Rails?**
>
> Rails has really evolved independently of our deployment needs, although as I said, I did write Capistrano to take care of that aspect. We've worked hard to make sure Capistrano plays nicely with Rails, and to that end Rails has changed a little bit to make that integration nicer. Things like the extensible Rake tasks were implemented as a consequence of the Capistrano integration work. But the design of Rails itself hasn't really been affected by deployment considerations, at least not significantly.
>
> We are using more or less the same underlying techniques that David used back when Basecamp was first released and Rails was being born. Thus, it might be more accurate to say that Rails and our deployment needs were born together, and the assumptions that Rails makes (and has always made) include some of those deployment assumptions. Take the directory layout that every Rails application uses—that assumes a few things about how your deployed application will look. However, the changes in Rails since its inception have not been significantly affected by deployment considerations.

Rails Schema Migrations

Often, the hard part about backing out a deployment is migrating your database backward in the event of a problem. Ruby on Rails uses a feature called *schema migrations* for the purpose. With schema migrations, Rails keeps a numbered list of migrations. Each migration has the ability to move up one level or back to the previous level. Then, developers can ask Rails to move to a particular migration version. If you move up, Rails applies the necessary migrations in order. If you move down, Rails backs out the migrations in reverse order.

Migrations help manage the schema, or structure of the database. (For example, you can add tables and indexes, rename columns or tables, or even remove columns from a database.) Migrations also migrate data. For example, if you added a greeting to a table called email_messages, you may want to initialize the greeting to Dear #{person.name}, which would personalize the greeting for each person in the database.

With the combination of version control software, Capistrano, and Rails migrations, you can provide a surprisingly sophisticated deployment strategy. In fact, your deployment strategy would likely be better than the strategy for many Java shops.

In this chapter, we looked at ramping up your development experience. In the next, we'll wrap up *From Java to Ruby* and tell you what you can expect in the next few years.

7.6 Executive Summary

- Ramping up to broad deployment is relatively new for Ruby.

- You can often draw from the Perl, Smalltalk, and Python communities to understand more about Ruby.

- You can expand the pool of available developers for Ruby projects.

- Capistrano and schema migrations are two features that simplify the deployment of Ruby applications.

- The deployment strategy of Ruby projects is often more advanced than similar Java project teams.

First rule of the kayak: When in doubt, paddle like hell
 ▶ unknown origin

Chapter 8

Risk

A kayaking guide once told me to "paddle like hell" in the heart of a rapid, because I'd have no chance of influencing the position of my boat if my paddle was not in the water. In software development, I've learned to paddle aggressively and with a purpose. If your software development is badly broken and your underlying technology is a big part of that problem, doing nothing is far more dangerous than taking a risk. I've written several books on fixing Java in evolutionary ways. But I've since come to believe that Java is simply not suitable for some types of problems. In many ways, this book, from cover to cover, is about risks worth taking.

But I've said many times throughout this book that adopting any new technology is a risky proposition. You can hurt yourself with any language, especially new languages like Ruby. In this chapter, we'll offer a concentrated discussion of the risks you will likely encounter along the way and some steps you can take to mitigate that risk.

8.1 Bad Risk

Good project management means avoiding bad risks and mitigating good risks, should you choose to take them. Not all risk is good risk. Any long-term technology manager knows this keenly. A high percentage of projects fail. Some reports[1] suggest as many as 80% of all software projects fail. Let's look at what makes a risk bad:

---

[1]http://www.standishgroup.com/sample_research/chaos_1994_1.php

- *Long odds.* The most obvious variable in risk is your odds of success. The greater your chance of failure, the better mitigation you'll need, and the higher payoff you'll require.

- *Payoff.* Some bad risks don't have any payoff at all. Working without backing up critical data at regular intervals is not a good risk because there's no payoff.

- *Need.* If you don't need the payoff, the risk is a bad one.

- *Consequence.* If the consequence of the risk is not proportionate to the reward, the risk is a bad one.

- *Accumulation.* Even low probabilities can accumulate to unacceptable levels. If you take too many big risks without effective mitigation, you will get burned.

- *Mitigation.* Most of the time, a major risk should require an effective backup plan.

- *The unknown.* What you don't know increases your risk.

Let's bring bad risks into context. Ruby is not the answer to every question. Certain scenarios have unacceptable risk as they relate to Ruby.

Not a Technology Problem

In general, you should solve your critical process problems before trying to attack ones based on technology. Most software development problems are not technology problems. Building the wrong software faster won't help. Solving systemic process or political problems should take precedence over a more productive programming language. A language won't change your work ethic. If you can't generate a payoff, the risk isn't worthwhile.

Admittedly, this process-first idea is an oversimplification, because a programming language can sometimes help your process flow more smoothly. For example, a language can help you shorten your cycle times and put solutions in front of your users more quickly. Shorter cycles and early feedback can be part of a broader process improvement. Still, process problems need to get attention first.

Political Opposition

Although some amount of political opposition to new languages appears inevitable, sometimes the opposition is so intense that you can't move your agenda forward. Depending on your potential reward, your ability to overcome the opposition, and the energy required to do so, you might decide to table Ruby adoption or choose one of the less-confrontational strategies we introduced in Chapter 4.

Not a Technical Fit

Ruby will make many good developers more productive and simplify many types of applications. You've seen that Rails is perhaps the most productive web development platform with broad circulation. Ruby has continuations and other features that Java doesn't, but not everyone needs Rails or continuations. Unless you need what Ruby offers, the risk will not be worthwhile.

Many technology problems come from choosing the wrong technology for the job. Ruby is going to excel at problems that demand a higher-level language. If raw processing power or hardware integration forms the foundation of your application, Ruby's higher-level structures are going to work against you. If you have a team that is dead set against automated testing, you probably need some of the additional safety nets that static languages provide, because they will catch at least some errors when your developers compile.

Similarly, Ruby won't have huge numbers of frameworks. If you're looking for full-stack web services to interoperate with WebSphere or .NET applications, you'd be better off relying on languages in tools supporting those platforms. Java's Swing may not be the most elegant framework in the world, but it is portable and rich. If you need to do fat-client development across platforms, Ruby may not be the answer.

Unknown Territory

Finally, some problems may or may not be fits for Ruby. These are some of the places that are breaking new Ruby ground:

- *Ultrahigh volume.* Although other dynamic languages have run some of the highest volume sites in the world, Ruby doesn't have such a flagship deployment yet.

- *Ultrahigh connections.* Massive numbers of concurrent users or requests have also not been proven.

- *Rich user interfaces.* Right now, most Ruby development is focused on web development, single-platform development, and integration scripts that don't have user interfaces.

I'm not suggesting that you run away from all risk, just that applying Ruby in such unknown territory increases your risk. If you find yourself in such a scenario, you may decide to gather more data (through possibly a prototype), you may decide to mitigate your risk, or you may decide that your combined risk level is unacceptable.

Dealing with Bad Risk

The knee-jerk reaction for dealing with bad risk is often to stop taking all risks. In software development, that mind-set can doom you to bleed to death slowly. Progress will move on with or without you. You're better off working to mitigate risk:

- *Gather information.* You've seen a heavy emphasis on pilot projects because they help you gather information about Ruby, often without staking too much on a given problem.

- *Create backup plans.* A backup plan doesn't reduce risk, but it does reduce the cost of failure. Running a Java project in parallel is an expensive backup plan, and identifying purchased software that you might buy if you fail is a cheaper one.

- *Scale back.* By scaling back your ambition, you can achieve something like 80% of the benefit with 20% of the risk. You can always add the remaining 20% in a later iteration.

- *Eliminate related risks.* If your accumulated risks go down, often the total risk level can become acceptable.

Risk mitigation is really turning bad risk into good risk. You'll use one of these strategies to mitigate each technical and political risk that you introduce.

8.2 Mitigating Technical Risk

A project manager for a new Ruby project must ultimately make the decision as to whether Ruby is technically up to the task. When you think of the risk of adopting a new technology, most people think about the technical risks first:

- Can the language do what I need it to do?

- Is it too buggy?

- Will it be fast enough?

- Can I train my people or find people who can use the new language?

- Can I get support?

When you are considering technical risks, you need to expand your assessment to include Ruby the language, the core Ruby frameworks you'll use, the Ruby programmers you'll use on the project, the Ruby community you'll tap to solve your problems, and the Ruby commercial industry that you'll tap to do your job. This world is not a Java world. The economics work differently in a few ways. It's an open source language with different licensing and economics (though Java depends on many open source projects too), it's a dynamic language that's easier to extend but less performant, and it's a newer language to the mass market, so there's less overall investment.

Open Source Projects

Working with minor open source projects is pretty straightforward. If the project does exactly what you need or if you can make it do what you need with minimal effort, you use it. If not, you move on to the next project or write the feature yourself.

Working with major, larger open source projects like Rails or the Ruby language is a different proposition. You'll sometimes depend on the community to make major enhancements, and you'll depend on the economy that springs up around the project to get the education, books and other media, recruits, and consulting you'll need to be successful. Open source projects can take risks that might be major for commercial projects and trim those risks to trivial levels, if your chosen project is successful.

So you should depend on Ruby, or some Ruby project, to the extent that you believe it will succeed. That's why I placed so much emphasis on momentum in Chapter 1. I do believe that Ruby will be wildly successful, powered by the success of it's flagship framework, Ruby on Rails.

Even so, the character of open source communities will change from project to project. From my experience, Ruby and Java differ dramatically in one primary way: open source contributions. The nature of the Ruby programming language leads to projects that are less complex and easier to extend. You'll find it much easier to make critical extensions to Ruby on Rails than to, say, Hibernate.

The Role of the community—A discussion with David Heinemeier Hansson

CTO, 37signals

Q: What's driving the rapid innovation in Rails?

Momentum comes from people needing something that's not there. Thus, if you needed composite keys, you could pour that momentum into a patch, rather than waiting for the community to solve your problems for you.

Q: What's the difference between the way your community's requirements are managed and the way they are managed on Java projects?

In the Java model, you would not even contemplate changing the frameworks. For example, Hibernate is something Gavin King does, and Struts has been frozen for years. The weight and complexity make it so.

But in the Ruby community, this is not so. It's so easy to extend and tweak the framework that anyone can do so and in a reasonable time period too. We have people coming to Ruby on Rails that contribute a patch on the first night of their journey.

So for a Java project, you may turn away from a project because Hibernate, Struts, or Spring doesn't do exactly what you need it to do. But Ruby gives you the ability to bend Active Record or Rails or even the language itself through patches. Then, it becomes a simple cost versus benefit analysis.

We encourage all Rails programmers to hop on and contribute to the project.

Building Risky Features

You can often effectively mitigate risk by attacking the riskiest element of a project first, while there's still time to recover. In one of my first Ruby on Rails development efforts, we had an inexperienced team and one high-risk element to cover. We needed to build an open-ended reporting engine. We decided to do reporting in our first iteration, rather than saving the feature until the last major drop. We got several benefits by attacking the risk early:

- We were able to give the customer a capability they did not have early in the project. Our early success made the customer much more cooperative.

- We were able to refine the interface, getting feedback from users earlier in the project.

- We got to see how the report writer would perform under load.

- When it became clear that we could handle about 70% of the customer's requests with a primitive engine, we changed the spec to include the minimal reporting engine, and the customer augmented our solution with a commercial report writer.

- The customer saved thousands on training and license fees by satisfying most needs through our tool.

We used three mitigation strategies: we attacked risk early, we built a backup plan, and we scaled back. We were successful only because we attacked the risk early enough to implement our fallback plan.

Reducing Coupling

You can often reduce your overall risk by reducing the coupling between the major pieces of your application. Rails makes this easy by enforcing a Model-View-Controller architecture. If you can reduce the size of the major components of your application, you can better survive major changes in strategy or design, because changes in one part of your application will not ripple through your entire system.

One of my long-standing Java customers built software for Wall Street. They knew that their customers needed a simplified development environment for web-based user interfaces but did not believe that their conservative customers would endorse Rails, because the framework required Ruby on the server.

In the end, we came up with a strategy that let the user build the user interface in the technology of their choice. We settled on a web services API, enabling access across multiple systems. We settled on ReST-based web services (see Chapter 6, *Bridges*, on page 95) for this purpose, enabling access from Ruby on Rails.

By decoupling the back end through web services and implementing a simplified ReST approach, the company can now sell its software to clients who are free to use Ruby on Rails. Their marketing reps can also build rapid demonstrations based on Ruby on Rails, which work much more quickly than their Java-based competition. They still get the full power of Java for their business engine, which has some enterprise integration requirements that are not well supported by Ruby.

Technical Prototypes

One of the most commonly employed risk mitigation techniques is the prototype. Technical prototypes help you learn. Several different companies have bucked conventional wisdom and employed Rails to solve problems that don't use the Active Record back end. These projects justified the use of Ruby on Rails based on an early prototype. Dynamic languages like Ruby make great prototyping languages, and Ruby on Rails includes additional features to make prototypes painless.

Automated Testing

Automated testing is a development practice in which developers build automated unit tests as they build code. The practice can make you more productive, and it's also a great tool for reducing your overall risk. Late changes are inevitable. At one account, we built an application with an extensive amount of native SQL on the PostgreSQL database engine. We chose it based on scalability and the absence of license fees.

As we negotiated with hosting vendors, we found that the best hosting company had only limited experience with PostgreSQL but extensive experience with MySQL. We were able to run the test suite and determine the total effort of supporting MySQL, down to the lines of code required, in only two hours.

Automated testing also mitigates risk in another way. Late changes to a code base are much riskier if you don't have the automated test suite to catch problems that you introduce. Ruby on Rails is a particularly good framework for automated testing. Rails builds in tools that make testing easy and organizes projects to make testing strategies consistent. Rails also builds in a test environment that makes tests almost painless to run.

Walking Away

Sometimes, when you've done all that you can to control a risk and you're still failing, you need to have the courage to walk away. Some teams will doubtlessly do better with Java than Ruby, and some problems are just not well suited to Ruby frameworks. Some teams, especially those with inexperienced programmers, will need more restrictive environments. When you've gathered your information and the answers are no, you need to listen and move on.

8.3 Mitigating Political Risk

Political risks imperil projects from a social perspective. New programming languages are especially prone to political risks because new languages will bring uncertainty and change. New languages also threaten skill sets and knowledge bases of your current staff and management. Where technical risks tax you by forcing you to work and cover details, political risks are difficult for a different set of reasons.

Handling Top-Down Risk

The most frustrating risk can be top-down risk. Convincing some managers to take a significant risk is a difficult proposition. The best way to combat such risks is to establish some early success. Chapter 4 showed you how to establish early pilots. One of the scenarios in that chapter, or a similar approach, might well be the ticket to your success. Still, even getting the green light to launch a pilot is often next to impossible. Here are some tips to move your agenda forward:

- *Sponsorship.* If you can find a sponsor in upper-management, your job gets much easier. The best sponsors have the most to gain from a successful transition.

- *Forgiveness rather than permission.* Sometimes, it's easier to ask for forgiveness than permission. You want to establish rapid value to offset the damage you do by moving forward without permission. This strategy works better in some companies than others, so know what the implications of success will be for you.

- *Alternative funding.* If you don't have to ask for additional budget, you can often start a pilot project without the support of upper-management.

- *Off-hours.* Sometimes you can convince employees to start a Ruby project after hours. Your hope is to compensate those developers once they establish success.

- *Dollars.* In the face of increasing financial pressures due to global competition, financial arguments become increasingly compelling. Usually, the capital you can save by reducing your cycle time by a mere fraction will lead to significant financial savings.

The key is persistence. If you get told no, think of it as the closing of just one path. Look for an alternate one. Once you've delivered your first successful application, you'll be surprised at how far your success will take you.

I recently worked on a Rails project where the upper-management gave the project only grudging support. We overcame objections by including that manager's most critical feature first. We put in a few extra hours to make sure that the Ruby solution delivered Ajax, which provided a much richer interface than the Java alternative. We turned a borderline enemy into an ally.

Managing Dissension, or Bottom-Up Risk

Good developers are passionate about what they do. The best developers love to choose sides. With a decision so huge as moving to Ruby, some programmers will definitely not support the project. So dissension is inevitable; you just need to manage it. These tips can help you deal with the inevitable dissension you'll face:

- *Be honest.* Most people are surprisingly accommodating when they know the whole story. If you need better productivity to survive, tell your people. If you think Ruby simply represents a better fit than what you're using, tell them that too.

- *Pick your leadership wisely.* Your long-term success often depends on who works on your initial pilots, because those people will be your most vocal leaders.

- *Build a broader community.* You will achieve better results long term though grass-roots growth.

At Amazon.com, a small Ruby group invited Dave Thomas to speak for several brown-bag education sessions over lunch and even worked to have Ruby installed on the new machines given to developers.

This early support led to a grassroots growth that whittled down internal dissension.

8.4   What's Ahead for Ruby?

Throughout this book, we've looked at the impact of moving people, programs, and organizations from Java to Ruby. In this last section, I'd like to play a short game of what-if. We'll look at two possible futures of Ruby.

First, let's take the darker scenario. What if Ruby does not get a major commercial investment? What if the growth tapers off and people decide that Ruby on Rails is not all things to all people? What will become of people who made a Ruby decision?

The Church of the Unthinkable

When I wrote *Beyond Java*, I suggested that Smalltalk would never be the next great language. I later reiterated this comment, saying that the Smalltalk train had rusted at the station, implying stagnation. I was not surprised by the outpouring of mail from developers defending their beloved language.

But I was surprised to find a vibrant, active community and an economy around it. The programmers understand that Smalltalk is not the next Java and probably never will be. A few major vendors told me their business was healthy and growing. In particular, James Robertson, an officer at Smalltalk vendor Cincom, had this to say:

Smalltalk likely won't become mainstream anytime soon, but I'd hardly refer to it as "rusted at the station." There are few profitable Java tool vendors. IBM is pressuring them with Eclipse, and once that's complete, there's a real danger that Eclipse will end up like Microsoft's Internet Explorer before the appearance of Firefox, with most of the funding dried up and stagnated.

Contrast that to Smalltalk, where we (Cincom) are profitable and our customer base is growing.

I've come to respect the Smalltalk programmer base. Sure, they'd like to see growth, but rather than bemoan what Smalltalk isn't, they celebrate what it is. Georg Heeg had this to say:

I just saw your article about Seaside. I love the picture of the "five times faster" "lightweight" "train rusted at the station." It is so wonderfully contradictory. It reminds me of the 27-year-old picture of "the craggy aloofness of the kingdom of Smalltalk...where great and magical things happen" [Byte Magazine, August 1978].

Indeed, within this vibrant and colorful community, strange and wonderful things do happen. The language is still incredibly productive, and people still use it with fantastic leverage to solve difficult business problems. And important innovation is still happening within that community. So the "unthinkable," stagnation, has happened to this quiet little community, but they're still devoted to the language, almost religiously.

I humbly suggest that in the worst-case scenario, Ruby may well wind up with a similar future. The culture, the language, and even the syntax are similar. Extreme productivity in a language that you can easily extend to meet your purposes: you could do worse.

Or an Explosion of Truth?

But I don't think we're headed for a future of obscurity or stagnation. Ruby has the catalyst that other dynamic languages have long been missing. I strongly believe that the dynamic object-oriented languages like Smalltalk, Ruby, and Python are a path to greater productivity. We are on the cusp of experiencing that increased productivity, for the first time, within a popular, commercially dominant language.

The programming mentors that I respect the most—including Martin Fowler, Dave Thomas, Stuart Halloway, and a few others—all tell me that dynamic languages have what we need to be more productive. We've been slowly moving toward a higher abstraction, from structured programming to object-oriented programming. A movement toward an interpreted dynamic language is the next logical step. And Ruby has the catalyst that a dynamic language will need to succeed. Ruby just feels right, like a fresh breath of pure truth.

A quick look at the excitement and controversy around Ruby and Rails should tell you that this beast is different. I haven't felt this kind of electricity since a medium-sized hardware company started a tiny little language in a laboratory, built it into a browser called Netscape, attached a mascot called Duke, and changed the name from Oak to Java.

Chapter 9

Bibliography

[Bro86]   Frederick P. Brooks, Jr. No silver bullet—essence and acci-
           dent in software engineering. *Proceedings of the IFIP Tenth
           World Computing Conference*, pages 1069–1076, 1986.

[DL99]   Tom Demarco and Timothy Lister. *Peopleware: Productive
           Projects and Teams*. Dorset House, New York, NY, second
           edition, 1999.

[GGA06]   Justin Gehtland, Ben Galbraith, and Dion Almaer. *Prag-
           matic Ajax: A Web 2.0 Primer*. The Pragmatic Programmers,
           LLC, Raleigh, NC, and Dallas, TX, 2006.

[HT00]   Andrew Hunt and David Thomas. *The Pragmatic Program-
           mer: From Journeyman to Master*. Addison-Wesley, Reading,
           MA, 2000.

[MIO98]   John D. Musa, Anthony Iannino, and Kazuhira Okumoto.
           Software Reliability: Measurement, Prediction, Application.
           McGraw Hill, New York, 1998.

[Moo99]   Geoffrey A. Moore. *Crossing the Chasm: Marketing and Sell-
           ing High-Tech Products to Mainstream Customers*. Harper-
           Business, 1999.

[Pin06]   Chris Pine. *Learn to Program*. The Pragmatic Programmers,
           LLC, Raleigh, NC, and Dallas, TX, 2006.

[Tat03]   Bruce Tate. *Bitter EJB*. Manning Publications Co., Green-
           wich, CT, 2003.

[Tat04]   Bruce Tate. *Better, Faster, Lighter Java*. O'Reilly & Asso-
           ciates, Inc, Sebastopol, CA, 2004.

[Tat05]   Bruce Tate. *Beyond Java.* O'Reilly & Associates, Inc, Sebastopol, CA, 2005.

[TFH05]   David Thomas, Chad Fowler, and Andrew Hunt. *Programming Ruby: The Pragmatic Programmers' Guide.* The Pragmatic Programmers, LLC, Raleigh, NC, and Dallas, TX, second edition, 2005.

Competitive Edge

Now that you've gotten an introduction to the individual practices of an agile developer, you may be interested in some of our other titles. For a full list of all of our current titles, as well as announcements of new titles, please visit www.pragmaticprogrammer.com.

Ship It!

Agility for teams. The next step from the individual focus of *Practices of an Agile Developer* is the team approach that let's you *Ship It!*, on time and on budget, without excuses. You'll see how to implement the common technical infrastructure that every project needs along with well-accepted, easy-to-adopt, best-of-breed practices that really work, as well as common problems and how to solve them.

Ship It!: A Practical Guide to Successful Software Projects
Jared Richardson and Will Gwaltney
(200 pages) ISBN: 0-9745140-4-7. $29.95

My Job Went to India

World class career advice. The job market is shifting. Your current job may be outsourced, perhaps to India or eastern Europe. But you can save your job and improve your career by following these practical and timely tips. See how to: • treat your career as a business • build your own brand as a software developer • develop a structured plan for keeping your skills up to date • market yourself to your company and rest of the industry • keep your job!

My Job Went to India: 52 Ways to Save Your Job
Chad Fowler
(208 pages) ISBN: 0-9766940-1-8. $19.95

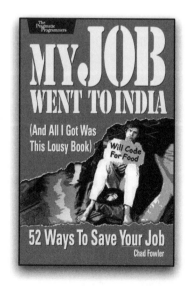

Cutting Edge

Learn how to use the popular Ruby programming language from the Pragmatic Programmers: your definitive source for reference and tutorials on the Ruby language and exciting new application development tools based on Ruby.

The *Facets of Ruby* series includes the definitive guide to Ruby, widely known as the PickAxe book, and *Agile Web Development with Rails*, the first and best guide to the cutting-edge Ruby on Rails application framework.

Programming Ruby (The PickAxe)

The definitive guide to Ruby programming.
• Up-to-date and expanded for Ruby version 1.8. • Complete documentation of all the built-in classes, modules, methods, and standard libraries. • Learn more about Ruby's web tools, unit testing, and programming philosophy.

Programming Ruby: The Pragmatic Programmer's Guide, 2nd Edition
Dave Thomas with Chad Fowler
and Andy Hunt
(864 pages) ISBN: 0-9745140-5-5. $44.95

Agile Web Development with Rails

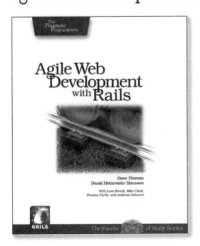

A new approach to rapid web development.
Develop sophisticated web applications quickly and easily • Learn the framework of choice for Web 2.0 developers • Use incremental and iterative development to create the web apps that users want • Get to go home on time.

**Agile Web Development with Rails:
A Pragmatic Guide**
Dave Thomas and David Heinemeier Hansson
(570 pages) ISBN: 0-9766940-0-X. $34.95

Visit our secure online store: http://pragmaticprogrammer.com/catalog

The Pragmatic Bookshelf

The Pragmatic Bookshelf features books written by developers for developers. The titles continue the well-known Pragmatic Programmer style, and continue to garner awards and rave reviews. As development gets more and more difficult, the Pragmatic Programmers will be there with more titles and products to help programmers stay on top of their game.

Visit Us Online

Java to Ruby Home Page
pragmaticprogrammer.com/title/fr_j2r
Source code from this book, errata, and other resources. Come give us feedback, too!

Register for Updates
pragmaticprogrammer.com/updates
Be notified when updates and new books become available.

Join the Community
pragmaticprogrammer.com/community
Read our weblogs, join our online discussions, participate in our mailing list, interact with our wiki, and benefit from the experience of other Pragmatic Programmers.

New and Noteworthy
pragmaticprogrammer.com/news
Check out the latest pragmatic developments in the news.

Save on the PDF!

Owning the paper version of this book entitles you to purchase the PDF version at a great discount. The PDF is great for carrying around on your laptop. It's hyperlinked, has color, and is fully searchable. Buy it now at pragmaticprogrammer.com/coupon

Contact Us

Phone Orders:	1-800-699-PROG (+1 919 847 3884)
Online Orders:	www.pragmaticprogrammer.com/catalog
Customer Service:	support@pragmaticprogrammer.com
Non-English Versions:	translations@pragmaticprogrammer.com
Pragmatic Teaching:	academic@pragmaticprogrammer.com
Author Proposals:	proposals@pragmaticprogrammer.com